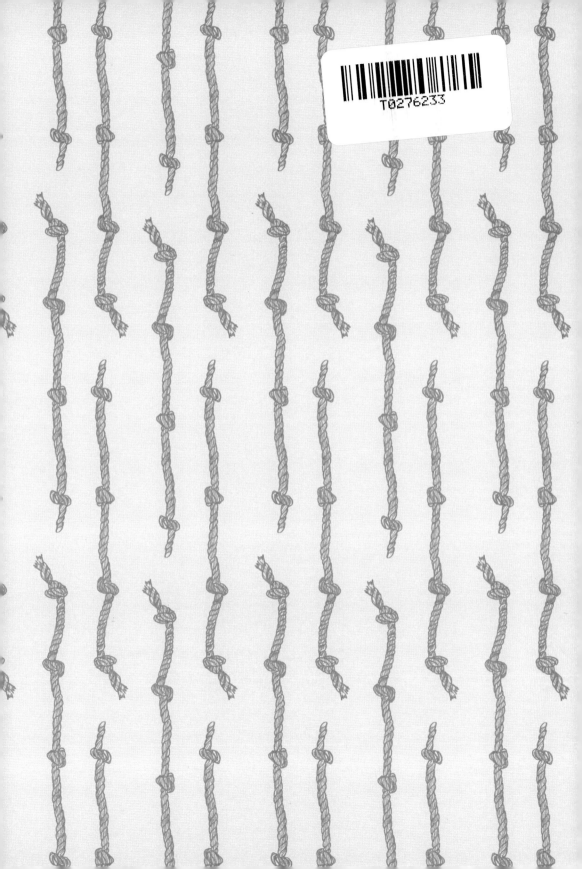

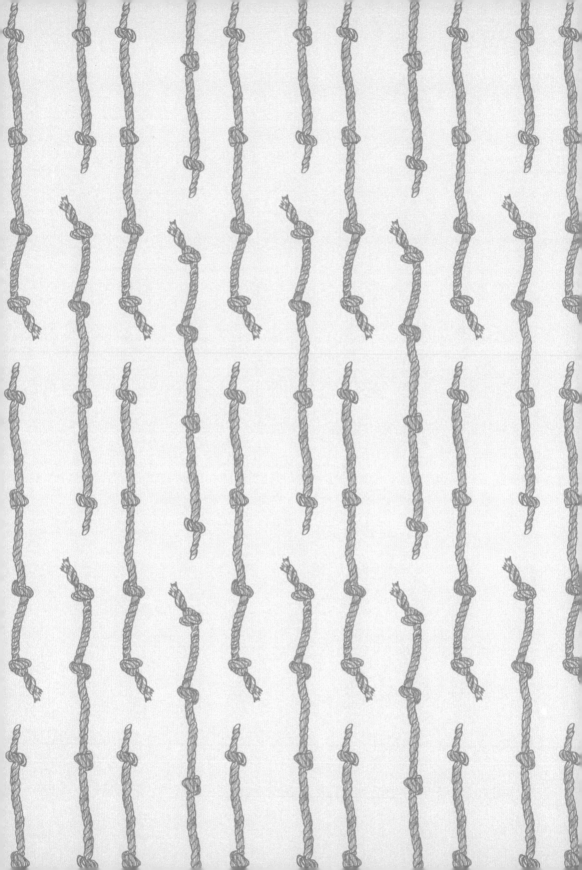

First published in Great Britain in 2023 by
Laurence King, An imprint of The Orion Publishing Group Ltd
Carmelite House, 50 Victoria Embankment
London EC4Y 0DZ

An Hachette UK company

10 9 8 7 6 5 4 3 2 1

A CIP catalogue record for this book
is available from the British Library.

ISBN 978-0-85782-905-4

Book and cover design by Alexandre Coco
Illustrations by David Sparshott
Project-managed by Rosanna Fairhead
Copy-edited by Sarah Yates
Proofread by Patricia Burgess
Americanized by Lisa Burnett Hillman
Indexed by Hilary Bird

Origination by F1 Colour Ltd
Printed in China by C&C Offset Printing Co. Ltd

www.laurenceking.com
www.orionbooks.co.uk

We dedicate this book to you,
Silvester, and we are looking
forward to everything you
bring us.

For safety, use caution, care, and judgment when following the procedures described in this
book. The authors and publisher cannot assume responsibility for any damage to property
or injury to persons as a result of the misuse of the information provided.
　　Always follow the manufacturer's instructions included with any tool or product. Some
sections of this book may require professional help by law. Consult your local building
department or planning office for information on building codes or regulations, permits,
and other laws as they apply to your project.
　　Be sure to use the correct size of tool for your fixing, and vice versa. Measurements
and sizes given in materials and tool lists are intended as guidance only. The treehouse on
which this book is based was built using metric measurements and tools, and conversions
to imperial may not be exact equivalents.

HOW TO BUILD A
TREEHOUSE

Christopher Richter & Miriam Rüggeberg

Laurence King Publishing

Before You Begin

Building the Substructure

Preparing the Site

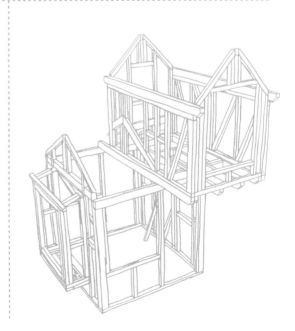

Building the Treehouse

Building the Interior

Special Features

Foreword
by Pete Nelson

Treehouses hold a certain magic that is recognized by young and old throughout the world. Whether it is the feeling a child gains when they climb a tree to a place that is all their own, or an adult's nostalgia when they behold a simple arboreal retreat, there can be no argument about the intrinsic positivity of a house in a tree.

As a young carpenter in the late 1980s I discovered that the wondrous feeling I had had as a child daydreaming about building an elaborate Tarzan-style treehouse in my backyard was alive and well. A neighbor had built a simple "tree fort" for his young son just down the street from where I lived, and it sparked a question that I have been striving to answer ever since: can human beings return safely and responsibly to the trees and forests of our beautiful world?

The personal journey that ensued has brought together builders, designers, engineers, and arborists, as well as ordinary people who simply love the notion of creating a simple space in the arms of nature—amateurs, like me, with a curiosity to see where our imaginations could lead us. Starting a treehouse-building company was no one's idea of a good business plan, but the joy it has brought to me and those around me is undeniable.

In 1997 I and some like-minded people organized the first World Treehouse Conference, which continues to this day. Our mission was to determine the safest way to connect structurally with living trees. Today, through the work of many people over many years, we have found a way to support our wildest dreams that keeps not only the treehouse occupants safe, but also the trees.

Perhaps the best parts of doing work you love are the relationships you gain through it. My dear friend Christopher Richter is a case in point. More than 20 years ago, his handsome face appeared just above the deck level of a small treehouse that I had started building in a Munich exhibition hall. He was head and shoulders taller than anyone around, and it dawned on me that my new friend had the natural attributes of a future treehouse-builder. Rarely have my instincts been so correct. With Christopher's help we won a gold medal at Exempla's Outdoor Architecture exhibition that year, and he and I have been friends and frequent international exchange students ever since.

In this book Christopher and his wife, Miriam, explain in detail how to go about planning and building safe, long-lasting tree-supported structures. As we forge ahead in this new genre of architecture, we are learning much about how trees respond to our heartfelt attention. Now, after decades of close observation, a healthy symbiotic relationship has developed between living trees and our whimsical builder spirits. Nothing beats spending time in nature, and if you can do it comfortably from a few meters above the forest floor, your connection with the natural world will only grow stronger.

To the trees!

Introduction

Picture this. Having nailed down the very last board, you put your hammer aside contentedly, take a step back, and survey the fruit of your labor. As you gaze at it, leaves are rustling gently, a soft breeze cools your face, and you hear birdsong. You let out a joyful sigh and a deep sense of peace washes over you. Refreshing drink in hand, you take a seat on a bench built with your own two hands and think, "Wow, I made that." What an amazing feeling!

The goal of this book is to help you achieve this deeply satisfying outcome. It is intended for all those who appreciate wood as a material, are good with their hands, and are not afraid of using tools. It will teach you how to build a simple but solid, top-quality treehouse, one that will be a joy for many years to come. It might be a parent-and-child project that finally gets built in the oak tree in the back yard, or the fulfillment of a long-held desire to create a refuge in nature.

Each treehouse is unique, of course, but we want to make things as easy as possible. To make sure that every step of the process is easy to follow, we built a treehouse at a friend's house, especially for this book. You can either copy this one exactly or use it as a template for a forest hideaway of your own. The structure of the book mirrors the shape of a tree: follow the main trunk up to the tiniest twig high in the treetop and it will show you, step by step, how to make a copy of the treehouse we built. The boughs and branches you encounter on your way up describe alternative methods. These are intended to help you implement any of your own ideas that differ from those of the treehouse we describe here.

The construction plan referred to throughout the book is available to download using the QR code on page 176, and we advise you to print it out. A 3D model of the treehouse is also available to download, and SketchUp (3D-design software) can be used to view and alter it. You can also use our model as a basic

☞ Several 3D-design software packages are available (including SketchUp, which we used to plan this treehouse) and these enable even beginners to draw up plans for DIY projects both small and large. Video tutorials for the relevant package will take users of all abilities through the key steps, and many programs are available in free versions (often with restricted functionality). It takes a little effort to get up to speed with digital design, but it will save you a lot of work on site. You can build a virtual treehouse and spot potential complications ahead, rather than encountering them during the build. Of course, you can also build your treehouse without digital help; the important thing is to be well prepared and equipped with suitable woods in the correct dimensions for each application. Combine that with the construction methods from this book and you will end up with a fantastic treehouse. A free version of SketchUp is available at www.sketchup.com.

design for your own treehouse and make any alterations to match your own ideas. Your local situation will no doubt look a bit different from ours, so we have included some alternative ways of attaching your construction, a selection of various substructures, the option for one or more stories, ideas for decorating the treehouse, and other special features, such as a zip line. You can work through each section of the book step by step or apply and adapt the methods we outline to your own project.

Resources

The book details the time, budget, and expertise required on our part to make this treehouse a reality, and you can use our parameters to get a better idea of these for your own project. Building a treehouse often means improvising, devising your own solutions, and responding flexibly to unexpected challenges. It is fundamentally different from many other projects that you might start in life, and you are likely to be in unfamiliar territory; a tree is a living thing that you have to accommodate and adapt to, so it's not unlike having a child. And speaking of children, this treehouse was the brainchild of head architect Leni (6 years old), who loves to play games in it with her brother Oskar. So thank you, Leni!

LABOR

Always make sure you have at least one person nearby to help during the build for a number of reasons: safety, additional fun (it's enjoyable doing things together), and practicality. There are quite a few things you just cannot do alone. As construction proceeds, you will need to call on others with increasing frequency to help you continue to build. You might manage to erect the substructure with just one assistant, but things get a lot more complicated as you move further up. When it's time for the walls, for example, you should definitely have four people on site: two below, to lift up the panels, and two above, to take and fit them. As you continue, it is always a good idea to have people working down on the ground and up on the platform at the same time; those on the ground can pass up tools and materials to those up high, and also take things down. For a project such as this, you should always have two or three helpers on call who can give you a hand if required.

TIME

We started building this treehouse in spring and finished in late summer. As we both have jobs and are parents to a small boy, we could build only at weekends. Work on the principle that construction will take longer than you think; bad weather, illness, and missing tools, not to mention mistakes and mishaps, can, and indeed will, delay the build. Make use of rainy days to prepare sections of the treehouse in the workshop or under shelter. If you can work only in fits and starts, you won't always be able to achieve the flow you need to get on properly, so try to build in fewer but longer sessions. This will enable you to work more efficiently and thereby achieve the desired results more quickly.

BUDGET

The cost of supplies for our treehouse amounted to about €3,500 ($4,000/£3,000). We used new materials throughout, except for the windows and ornamental boards on the handrail. All the sections exposed to the weather are made from larch, which is expensive; the interior is made exclusively out of cheaper spruce. We would not recommend choosing spruce for the exterior sections since the need for it to be treated would quickly reduce any savings, and the required regular reapplications of treatment would cut down savings further still. Treated spruce does not look half as attractive as larch, not to mention the environmental impact of the treatment process itself. So how do you cut down on costs? Get ahold of as many second-hand materials as you can: old windows, repurposed boards and joists, or even corroded corrugated-iron sheeting to cover the roof will give your treehouse a lived-in look. You will be sparing both your wallet and the environment. Make sure that any reused wood is in good condition and any metal is not rusted through. Borrow expensive tools or rent them from a hardware store or tool-rental center, as a lot of the equipment you will use might never be needed again.

Why trust us?

Christopher is a freelance designer and builder of treehouses with a proud track record of more than 200 professional builds, each one unique, under the name Baumbaron (Tree Baron). He knows the entire process like the back of his hand, from coming up with the initial concept and figuring out all the planning stages, to adding the last shingle. He also knows how important it is to have a properly thought-out plan for

Christopher and our son
Silvester drilling a hole.

the treehouse to be solid and long-lasting. He never had a treehouse of his own as a child, which might be the cause of his insatiable desire to build them now. After he spent some time with the master treehouse-builder Pete Nelson in the United States, his fate was sealed: he knew that working among trees was the life for him, and he could never forgo the smell of cedar shingles. In 2013 he began his treehouse blog to create a space where anyone with an interest in building could find all kinds of fascinating stories about treehouses. He went on to fall in love with Miriam, who shares his enthusiasm for treehouses, and if all their dreams come true, they will eventually have a treehouse of their own one day.

Miriam, as a child, enjoyed climbing fruit trees in the backyard. When she wasn't reading up in a tree, occasionally doing vocabulary homework, or picking apples, she was teaching local rescue cats how to climb trees. When she was 12, a carpenter friend helped her build her own treehouse, which was nicknamed the "robbers' den." Alongside a scary sign, she suspended the bare ribs of an umbrella from the roof joist like a giant spider to frighten away unwelcome guests. In her guise as a pirate (or occasionally an orphan child spirited away by a witch), she would read and sleep there, inviting all the neighborhood cats in for milk and the "fish" she imagined catching over the side. For her, the treehouse was a blank space she could fill with her free-ranging imagination, wild adventures,

and fantastic stories. Later in life, Miriam turned her passion for writing into a career, and she now works as a freelance editor and blogger. Her fascination with treehouses has continued to grow, and as if all that were not enough, she also fell in love with a treehouse-builder. Together, Miriam and Christopher have a tool-crazy son and a blog at www.treehouseblog.com.

Building a treehouse with children

  If you choose to build a treehouse with one child or more, never leave them unsupervised with tools. Provide them with protective equipment and, if they are a little older, with good-quality tools. Small children will be happy to use play tools.

One volunteer is worth ten pressed men, as the old adage says. Involve the child and take on board their wishes and inclinations; give them agency in their jobs by offering an age-appropriate range of options for them to choose from: "Would you prefer to screw down some boards or help me sand down the handrail?" This way, the child will feel a sense of control and be even more enthusiastic about helping build the treehouse. Each section contains suggestions for ways in which you can playfully involve them in the construction process. As a parent or guardian, you will of course be the best judge of each job you can let your child take charge of, and which tools they are allowed to use.

If you have faith in the child and entrust them with responsibility, they will be more confident in the future. Let them gain some experience (under your supervision) and even make a few mistakes. Part of this process may involve hitting the occasional finger with a hammer before they fully appreciate the need to be careful with tools. Encourage them and remind them that things get a little bit better each time. They will discover that a skill is a learning process involving more than just natural talent.

Every child learns at his or her own pace, and it is worth remembering that children have less perseverance and shorter attention spans than adults do. If your child is tired or unable to finish a job, try not to be angry but instead shrug it off. Doing otherwise runs the risk of them losing their sense of enjoyment in building the treehouse and they may come to see it as a chore, which would be a shame. The joy of building should always come first. Working with a deadline will be stressful for both you and your child, so make sure you allow enough time.

Your little one(s) can of course work on their own projects, such as making a small chair, doing a bit of carving, painting a door sign, etc. Leave space for their own ideas and try not to offer too many tips and opinions of the "you should do it like this instead" kind. You could avoid commenting at all unless safety is at risk. We suggest a few ideas for child-friendly tasks throughout the book.

Admire the child's work and thank them for helping you so well. We can't stress enough how important it is not to make judgments or criticize their work. Like every child, each project is unique and individual.

How to use this book

Hang on a second! Before you get going, take a moment to discover the best way to work with this book. Read through the instructions carefully, all the way to the end. They contain important legal information about building a treehouse, and on-site health and safety precautions, along with lots of other hints and tips that you will find handy as you proceed. We have put together a summary of all the tools and materials you will need for your treehouse in Chapter 1. Subsequent chapters deal with actually building the treehouse and are structured as follows:

SECTION HEADING. Each section introduction outlines the steps described in that section and what you should pay special attention to.

TOOLS. Here is where we list the tools you will need to complete the procedures described in the section. We don't mention standard tools, such as a folding ruler, pencil, or cordless drill, every time; these are grouped under Basic Equipment (see page 22) and you should always have this kit handy.

MATERIALS. This is where you can check which building materials (such as wood, screws, or flashing) are required at this stage. If you are designing the treehouse yourself, you can check which lumber (timber) dimensions are suitable for each building stage, although there are exceptions for the platform and the substructure; see "Planning and sizing load-bearing beams" on page 35.

WHAT TO DO IN THE WORKSHOP. Here you will discover the preparatory work that is easier to do on the ground (such as cutting and preparing individual workpieces).

WHAT TO DO ON SITE. Under this heading you will find the steps required for installing work on site.

This book will guide you through the project as thoroughly and helpfully as possible. You should also have the confidence to put it to one side, however, and follow your instincts, until you hit a problem and turn back to the book again.

Like with baking a cake, where it is essential to read the whole recipe before starting, it is important to read the relevant treehouse sections all the way to the end. This will give you a good overview of the work ahead and an idea of all the important details. It will also save you a lot of effort. OK—let's get to those trees!

This book is a step-by-step guide to building a treehouse. In addition to carpentry techniques, it describes methods that have proved their worth in more than 200 treehouse projects of every shape and size that we have completed over the years. This makes it easy for beginners to use and/or for those wanting to build smaller treehouses.

1
Before You Begin

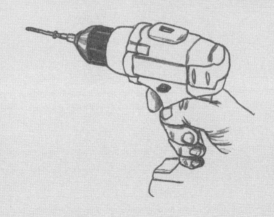

1.1
Safety first!

For safety reasons, you should do all the work described in groups of two or more and always under the supervision of at least one adult.

Particularly dangerous tasks, such as operating electric saws, should be carried out only after proper training by a qualified person. Always take safety precautions when working at height, using either a railing or suitable protective equipment—including a helmet and harness—to prevent falls.

It is important to remember that working with wood can be dangerous. Always exercise care when using tools and, especially when working with power tools, read the instruction manual first and follow the health and safety directions. Wear suitable clothing: no baggy shirts that could get in your way as you work, or flip-flops that leave feet exposed to unnecessary danger. If your hair is longer than shoulder length, tie it back so it won't get caught when you are drilling or sinking screws. The blades and drill bits of your tools should always be sharp for precision and safety.

From the first to the last moment of your treehouse build, health and safety are paramount: your own, that of your assistants/team, and that of your tree. See Tree Health (pages 31–2) for guidelines.

The ten commandments for building a treehouse

1. **Always be careful when working, and think twice about what you are doing before every step.**

2. **Look out for each other.**

3. **Don't run. Don't rush.**

4. **Keep your work area clean and free of trip hazards or objects that can fall from a height.**

5. **Wear suitable protective clothing (solid work boots, gloves, helmet).**

6. **Only do work that you feel is completely safe, particularly at height.**

7. **Pull the plug before changing a drill bit or saw blade, for example.**

8. **Always work in a group of at least two on site.**

9. **It's better to continue the next day than "just quickly finish" something today; things done in a rush tend to need redoing later.**

10. **Good planning prevents poor performance; every additional task and extra trip to the hardware store will waste time unnecessarily.**

1.2
Setting up your work area

Make sure everything is set up and that you have the required tools and materials handy before starting work.

POWER SUPPLY. The power for your work area will probably come from an electric socket somewhere in the house, shed, or backyard. If there is no socket nearby, you could use a suitable generator, although this will result in constant noise and smell, so resort to this solution only with caution. Depending on the distance between the power outlet and your work area, you will need one or more heavy-duty extension cords. These (and all the cords/cables you use) must be suitable for outdoor use. Always unroll the extension cord reel completely so that the cord does not overheat when in use, and if you are using a compressor, plug it in as close as possible to the power source so that it gets enough power to start. It's best to tie the ends of your extension cords together loosely wherever they connect, so you don't lose power suddenly in the middle of a job.

PLUGGING IN YOUR CHARGERS. Each day, before starting your build, plug in your chargers to make sure you always have full batteries. It would be annoying to have to interrupt your work because you've forgotten such a basic task.

SETTING UP WORK SURFACES. It's an excellent idea to set up two trestles with a large wooden board on top as a workbench on which to prepare components and workpieces at a comfortable height. It is also somewhere to put your tools. Two benches would be ideal: a large one to work on and a small one for your equipment. A wallpaper hanger's pasting table, for example, would suffice, and you'll get a lot of space for not much money. Even better if you can hang a large tarp as a protective cover over your work surface.

STORING MATERIALS. Beams, boards, braces, or bars—store all your building materials properly before use. This means ensuring they are protected from moisture and are well ventilated to prevent mold. Place sleepers under your materials to lift them off the ground, or put your lumber (timber) on trestles. You should also make sure that there is a gap between your pieces of wood by placing small spacers between each layer. If you are working with roofing film and/or roof panels, use them or a large and robust construction tarp (the woven tarps edged with metal eyes, available from home-improvement/DIY stores) to protect your materials from rain, making sure that enough air can still get to your wood. Fungus and mold will form quickly if the wood is stored in airtight packaging. Weigh down the cover to keep it from flying off in strong winds.

RAIN PROTECTION. Keep a tarp handy to cover your tools safely in the event of a sudden rain shower. Alternatively, put them into a large aluminum box, which can also be used to carry large quantities of tools back and forth.

BASIC EQUIPMENT. Standard tools, such as your folding ruler, pencils, and cordless drill, are grouped as basic equipment in the tools list on page 22. Always have these tools on site.

FOOTINGS. If using quick-setting concrete for your foundations, you can continue working the same day. With standard cement, however, you may need to wait two or three days until it has set, or there is a danger that the foundation will crack and you will have to start from scratch. Either way, you will need a dust mask, because the dust thrown up while using cement is harmful to your lungs. Use gloves, too, as the dust is also bad for your skin and will dry it out.

1.3
Choosing your wood

We have found larch and spruce to be good species of wood for treehouses; both are available from lumber (timber) yards and home-improvement stores.

Larch should be your first choice for wherever the wood is to be exposed to the elements. Thanks to its high resin content, it is highly weather-resistant and does not have to be treated; protecting the wood through construction measures (arrangement of woodgrain, etc.) will be sufficient. Load-bearing elements, such as the substructure and platform, can be made entirely out of larch.

Spruce is highly suitable for building wall frames and roof trusses. It is relatively inexpensive and easy to work with as it is a very soft wood. It should be used *only* for the interior, however, otherwise it will have to be pretreated with wood preservatives.

There are of course countless other species of wood that are particularly suitable for interiors and furniture. See the Sources section (pages 168–71) for lots of helpful books on working with different woods.

A large knot in the wood (such as the one in the illustration below) will considerably weaken your workpiece at that point. Your wood should never look like this, especially if it is going to be load-bearing. It needs to be as knot-free as possible. Small knots are no problem, however.

Constructive wood protection

To avoid the use of chemicals, a couple of simple design-based technical precautions will help you protect the parts of your treehouse that are exposed to the weather.

End grain, i.e. a face that has been cut perpendicular (at 90 degrees) to the grain, should never be installed horizontally on the exterior of the structure. A small inclination of 5 degrees will let water flow away much more efficiently and make sure that the places where water might penetrate especially easily cannot become waterlogged. A small roof over a horizontal end-grain face will also provide good protection.

Windowsills should not be installed exactly horizontally, but with a slight incline that allows water to flow outward. A small horizontal channel on the underside of the windowsill will act as a *drip groove*, ensuring that water drips off underneath before it can run back toward the wall and find a way into the house.

Sufficiently large *eaves* oversailing by at least 6in (15cm) will protect both windows and façade.

Always install uprights and ladders with a *gap between the wood and the ground*. Using post anchors will allow you to achieve sufficient spacing of at least 6in (15cm) between the ground and your wood. This will prevent patches of rot developing in this critically important area.

Make sure there is sufficient *ventilation* behind the outer skin, i.e. the cladding of your treehouse. With an uninsulated treehouse, this is a given and nothing more needs to be done, but if you have an insulated treehouse, the outer skin will have to be mounted on battens. A second, waterproof layer should be fitted under the battens to protect the insulation material from moisture.

1.4
Planning permission

Whether you require planning or zoning permission for a treehouse will largely depend on its size and the nature of its intended use.

There is a maze of different regulations, according to which country and state or county you live in. It is essential to get in touch with the local authorities if you want a definitive answer to this question. If you are building an uninsulated treehouse, such as the one shown in this book, it is generally enough to get your neighbors' approval.

Laws vary from place to place, but you should always bear the following points in mind.

KEEP YOUR DISTANCE. The treehouse should be away from neighboring properties or, if an acceptable distance is impossible, under a certain height, depending on local regulations. Keep in mind that this height is usually measured from the ground, rather than applying only to the height of the treehouse structure itself. There is often a difference in regulation between treehouses that are purely play houses and those that are to be permanent.

DO NOT EXCEED THE MAXIMUM SIZE. In most places, planning permission is generally not required for treehouses up to a certain size (once again, check whether the empty space under the treehouse is included). Consult the relevant authorities and/or do some online research to establish the regulations in your area.

ASK YOUR NEIGHBORS. Any neighbor will be delighted to be asked for consent before a building project is started, and this is especially the case if your treehouse might affect them personally in some way, perhaps by blocking their view or overlooking their bedroom or the like. Be transparent when showing neighbors your plans, and ask them to be understanding; if it turns out later that your treehouse is in a legal grey area, you will then have the neighbors on your side and a better case should there be objections from the authorities. Such objections generally tend to stem from neighbors, so forewarned is forearmed.

THE GREAT OUTDOORS. If you intend to build your treehouse in the wild (out in the woods, for example), rather than in your backyard or on land where building is permitted, things will get difficult. This is largely prohibited unless there are already buildings on the site in question, and even then you are very unlikely to get approval from the relevant authorities.

1.5
Tools

This section gives an overview of the tools you will require for your project and/or those we used to build our own. You might need a few more, but this will depend on your design. (Numbers in bold refer to the illustrations.)

You may be lucky enough to find one or two tools in good condition second-hand. They often sit gathering dust for years before ending up in the want ads (classifieds) or garage sales, or on online auction sites. It's worth keeping your eyes and ears open. You can also rent many of the tools in the list below from hardware stores or tool-rental centers, or you may know someone who can lend you some hardware for your project, if you let them help you with it. Some recommended tool suppliers are listed on page 171, but ask around to find the trusted sources in your area.

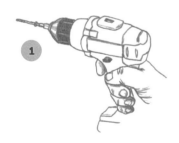

Safety equipment

Hearing protection

Eye protection

Rubberized work gloves

Helmet

Climbing gear (harness, rope, etc.)

First aid kit

MATERIALS TO PROTECT YOUR TREE

Woodchips or bark mulch to protect the roots

Tarps or drop cloths (dust sheets) to protect the bark

Power tools

ESSENTIAL

2 or 3 cordless drills, at least 18V and >4 Ah   **1**

Plenty of bits; it's best to work with the Torx™ (star) system, and you will need at least sizes T15, T20, T25, T30, and T40

Correct screws (see page 21), not Phillips or slotted screws

Jigsaw

Miter and circular table saw (you can get these two in one, as a combination tool)

Circular saw

Chainsaw (cordless or gas/petrol-powered)

Hammer drill

Angle grinder   **2**

Orbital sander (plus 60, 80, 120 grit sanding discs)

Belt sander (plus 60, 80, 120 grit belts)

NICE TO HAVE

Pneumatic nail gun (air nailer), plus compressor   **5**

Plane

Impact screwdriver

Oscillating saw, panel saw, and plunge saw

Router (plus various router bits)

DISTO laser distance meter

Nibbler

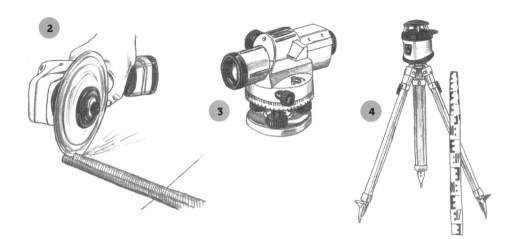

Hand tools

ESSENTIAL

Handsaw, tenon saw, or Japanese saw

Set of chisels (plus mallet)

Claw hammer

Block plane

Ratchet wrench (plus 1⅞in/46mm socket)

Rubber mallet (ideally dead blow)

Screw clamps

Wood glue (polyurethane or D4), suitable for outdoor use (we have had good results with products made by Titebond and Beko)

Hammer tacker

Utility knife (Stanley knife)

Tin snips

Waterproof duct tape

Socket set

Crimping tool   **6**

For measuring

Levels (spirit levels), long and short

Tape measure (25ft/8m)

Folding ruler

Carpenter's pencils

Carpenter's square

Carpenter's angle measuring tool

Combination square

Compass with pencil-holder

Sliding bevel

Plummet/plumb bob

Water level or surveyor's level   **3,4**

For digging

Spade

Shovel

Pickaxe

Trowel

Mortar tub or large bucket

Mixing attachment for power drill

Site equipment

Ladder(s), extension ladder (minimum 20ft/6m), and stepladder

Scaffolding

Extension cord reel(s)

Extension cord

Wooden trestles

Rope to haul up loads (minimum load capacity 660lb/300kg)

Pulley(s) and pulley blocks

Lashing straps

Wheelbarrow

Large tarp(s)

Zinc galvanizing spray

Garbage bags

Push (road) broom

Dustpan and brush

The most important saws

The following types of saw are most suitable for shaping (i.e. cutting and sizing) the individual elements of your treehouse, assuming you don't intend to fashion it with just an axe, hacksaw, and drawknife. Here is a brief introduction to each type:

MITER SAW

Using a miter saw is the quickest and most precise way of cutting the many parts of a treehouse to size; you can set the angle directly and it will always make a clean cut (generally perpendicular to the grain). The rotating table allows you to make mitered cuts of at least -45 degrees to +45 degrees, and the saw blade can be angled in either direction. Many miter saws have

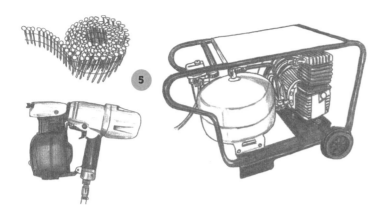

an integrated stop that will work for long workpieces, so you don't even need to measure or mark. When working with a miter saw, use only workpieces 6in (15cm) or more in length to make sure they are properly seated on the table and can't be grabbed and thrown across the room by the rapidly rotating saw blade. Always hold the workpiece securely, keeping your hands at least 6in from the saw blade.

PANEL SAW OR CIRCULAR TABLE SAW

A panel saw is the most suitable tool for making rip cuts (cutting your workpiece to the desired width, usually parallel to the grain); as the name suggests, it is also intended for cutting panels. Few people will have access to such a large, specialized device, however, so the second-best (but still very good) option for lengthwise cutting is a circular table saw. The blade of both types of machine can be inclined up to 45 degrees, thereby enabling angled cutting. When ripping longer workpieces on a circular table saw, you should always work with a partner so that one person can stand behind the saw to receive and hold the workpiece. When working with these tools, never push the workpiece into the saw blade with

bare hands; always use a push stick to make sure there is a safe distance between the blade and your hand (which will be grateful to you for taking such trouble).

PLUNGE SAW WITH GUIDE RAIL, OR CIRCULAR SAW

Rip cuts and cross-cuts can also be made effectively with a plunge saw. On a treehouse build, this type of saw is particularly useful for trimming platform boards after laying them. Cutting out apertures for windows and doors (and all other rip cuts) is also extremely easy to do by hand with a plunge saw. You will never want to be without this tool once you have used it. Mark two points, lay down a fence (guard), and away you go with your cut. You can also use a plunge saw to start a cut on the workpiece and then plunge the saw; this is handy for cutting slots, for example. A circular saw without a plunge function is a simpler and thus more affordable type. It is also available with a fence and should be part of every treehouse-builder's basic equipment. The blades of both types of saw can be inclined up to 45 degrees, making angled cutting possible.

⚠️ With every saw, make sure you are using the right blade. There are different ones for rip cuts and cross-cuts.

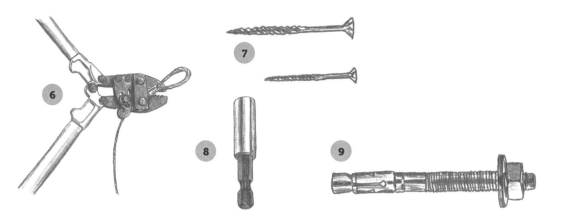

Fixings and fasteners

WOOD SCREWS WITH TORX HEAD   7

Stainless steel
#4×¾in (3×20mm)
#8×1¼in (4×30mm)
#8×1½in (4×40mm)
#8×2in (4×50mm)
#10×2⅜in (5×60mm)
#10×2¾in (5×70mm)
#12×4in (6×100mm)
#12×4¾in (6×120mm)

Waferhead screws
#12×2in (6×50mm)

Self-tapping screws
#10×2in (5×50mm)

Roofing (Spengler) screws

Hex screws
¼×4in (8×100mm) or ½×4in (10×100mm)

Galvanized
#12×4in (6×100mm)
#12×4¾in (6×120mm)
#12×5½in (6×140mm)
#12×7⅞in (6×200mm)
#12×8⅝in (6×220mm)
#12×9½in (6×240mm)

Countersunk screws
#5×2in (3.2×50mm)

Casement catches

OTHER SCREWS

Specialist tree attachment bolt/treehouse screw (tree lag bolt) plus bracket

NAILS

Stainless steel
Coil nails: 2½in (65mm) (US size 8d)

Galvanized
Coil nails: 2½in (65mm) (US size 8d)
Clout nails/felt tacks: ¾in (20mm)
Annular ring nails/ring shanks: 2in (50mm) (US size 6d)

CARRIAGE BOLTS/ THREADED RODS

M6 carriage bolts: 5½in (140mm)

M12 carriage bolts: 8in (200mm) and 8⅝in (220mm)

M12 threaded rods: 9½in (240mm)   **10**

Suitable washers and nuts

Suitable ring nuts   **11**

M10 express anchor   **9**

DRILL BITS

Wood drill bit set ⅛–½in (3–12mm)

Auger bits: ½in (12mm) and 1⅜in (36mm)

1¼in (30mm) Forstner bit

3in (74mm) Forstner bit with 1⅜in (36mm) shank

Screw starters with countersink: ⅛in (4mm), ³⁄₁₆in (5mm), and ¼in (6mm)

⅜in (10mm) masonry drill bit

Bit holder   **8**

JOIST HANGERS

4¼×4¼in (110×110mm)

2¼×4in (60×100mm)

2¼×4¾in (60×120mm)

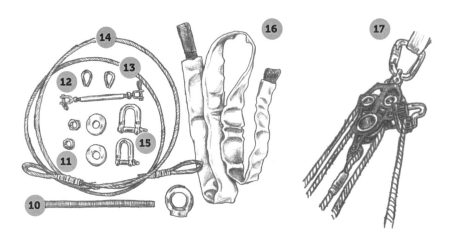

MISCELLANEOUS

Make sure all the following have the correct load-bearing capacity for the job.

$^{7}/_{16}$in (12mm) wooden dowels

Stainless-steel turnbuckles/bottle screws **12**

Stainless-steel shackle **13**

Stainless-steel cable $^{1}/_{4}$in (6mm) **14**

Thimbles $^{1}/_{4}$in (6mm) **15**

Loop strap **16**

Hinges/gate hinges for door (and windows if building your own)

L-shaped post anchor

Height-adjustable post anchor

BASIC EQUIPMENT

You should always have the following tools on hand, whatever stage of the build you are tackling:

Safety equipment (see page 18)

Folding ruler

Tape measure (25ft/8m)

Pencil

Utility knife (Stanley knife)

Cordless screwdriver and bit set

Wood drill bit set $^{1}/_{8}$–$^{1}/_{2}$in (3–12mm)

Screw starter with countersink

Handsaw

Circular saw

Claw hammer

Screw clamps

Wood glue

Socket set

Levels (spirit levels), long and short

Combination square

Ladder(s), extension ladder (at least 20ft/6m), and stepladder

Extension cord reel(s)

Extension cord

Wooden trestles

Rope to haul up loads (minimum load capacity 660lb/300kg)

Pulley(s)

Pulley blocks **17**

Large tarp(s)

Garbage bags

Push (road) broom

Dustpan and brush

1.6
Materials

Here is a summary of all the materials you will need (sizes and numbers will differ for each project). If you can, use good-quality, environmentally friendly or second-hand materials that are in good condition. This will allow you to enjoy your creation for years to come, and your conscience will be equally happy.

Wood

You can buy wood from a sawmill, lumber yard (timber merchant), or home-improvement (DIY) store. Make sure that the wood is of the dimensions stated. Our treehouse was designed and built using solid structural timber, and all dimensions quoted in the book and on the construction plan refer to this. Solid structural timber means that the joists and beams have been thicknessed and planed to exact dimensions and have a maximum moisture content of 15–18 percent. You will need:

105ft (32m) of larch beams (4×4in/11×11cm) for the substructure *or* 40ft (12m) of larch beams (4×4in/11×11cm) for the alternative substructure with robinia logs *or* 125ft (38m) of larch beams (4×4in/11×11cm) for the alternative substructure with four uprights (no tree)

138ft (42m) of larch beams (2×4in/6×12cm) for the substructure and upper floor

2 × 10ft (3m) larch boards (2×8in/5×20cm) for the ship's ladder

112ft (34m) of larch battens (3×3in/7×7cm) for the handrail, etc.

290ft (88m) of larch boards (1×6in/2×14cm, planed or unplaned) for the cladding

46ft (14m) of larch boards (1×8in/2×19cm, planed) for the handrail boards

158ft (48m) of larch boards (1×8in/2×19cm, planed) for the porches

276ft (84m) of larch boards (1×8in/2.5×19cm) for the floor and handrail boards

(230ft/70m of larch battens, 1×2in/25×45mm, if you wish to fill in the spaces beneath the handrail)

565ft (172m) of spruce beams, solid structural timber (2×2in/6×6cm), for wall framing, rafters, etc.

190ft (58m) of spruce beams, solid structural timber (2×4in/6×12cm), for wall framing, upper floor, purlins, etc.

Spruce boards ¾in/20mm for 140ft² (13m²) roof boards

(Roof battens 1×2in/30×50mm, if you wish to use battens when fitting the roof)

Interlocking (tongue-and-groove) floorboards 1in/25mm for 38ft² (3.5m²) of upper floor

If you choose to build the substructure with robinia logs:

2 robinia logs of about 6–8in (16–20cm) diameter, about 10ft (3m) long

2 robinia logs of about 4–6in (12–14cm) diameter, about 8ft (2.5m) long

Roof

Roofing underlay (film) or roofing felt

Corrugated (box-profile) sheeting

Windows

Vintage windows from flea markets, antiques stores, want ads (classifieds), or online auctions

If making your own: Plexiglas, ideally impact-resistant (e.g. Makrolon™)

Miscellaneous

Fast-setting (quick-mix) or standard concrete

We built the treehouse shown in this book exactly as described. The images illustrate the steps we followed and the captions provide all the information you need. When describing each stage, we always refer to the construction plan downloadable using the QR code on page 176. If you are designing your own treehouse, ignore our dimensions and apply the basic methodology to your project. Since your treehouse is likely to look different from ours, we have featured alternative installation methods (see 3.1, 3.7, and 3.8). You can use these if, for example, your tree has grown differently from the way ours has, or if you have several trees (or none).

2
Preparing the Site

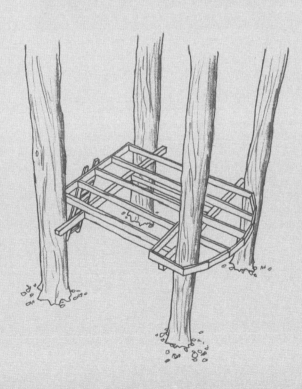

2.1
Attaching the treehouse

In addition to showing you how to construct a treehouse, this book explains everything you need to know about the most reliable methods of attaching it to the tree, or supporting it more generally. There are three such methods, and they are:

1. MOUNTING it on the tree using a treehouse attachment bolt (TAB).

2. HANGING it from the tree using a loop strap and steel cable.

3. SUPPORTING the treehouse from the ground with posts on spot footings. This method does not involve making a direct connection to the tree but belongs here as it is often used in combination with the other methods.

One tree, several trees, or no tree?

You can combine the methods above or use just one (whichever makes most sense for your treehouse). The method(s) you ultimately decide on will largely depend on the tree(s) in which you wish to build. Deciding factors will be species, size, and condition. Our instructions assume that the trees are healthy, robust, and suitable for bearing the weight of a treehouse.

Let's run through the three possible scenarios to help you choose the best method of attaching your treehouse.

1. NO TREE. An open-and-shut case: in the absence of a tree in which to build, you will be working exclusively with posts. See section 3.7 for a description of the substructure, which outlines a possible approach in these circumstances.

2. ONE TREE. A tree with a diameter of about 20in (50cm) can be used as the sole support for your treehouse if it is attached with treehouse attachment bolts. If the diameter is smaller, you should plan to add posts. If the tree features suitable parts from which you can also hang elements of the treehouse (see 3.3), you can use this method as well, for extra security. You should always adapt the dimensions of the treehouse to the size of the tree to avoid overloading it. For more on this topic, see section 2.4.

3. SEVERAL TREES. The minimum diameter of each tree can be a little smaller in this case. Treehouse attachment bolts can be used on trees with a diameter greater than about 16in (40cm). The thicker the trees, the better, as they will move less in the wind. Additional hanging points will allow you longer cantilevers and enable you to distribute the weight across several points. You can add posts here if the structure of the tree requires them. See section 3.4 for an explanation of the factors that decide this.

☞ The distance between your trees should always be between 10 and 20ft (3–6m). A shorter distance will leave you with little usable space, since you will still have to plan in the eaves and the clearance between the treehouse and the tree. A greater distance will mean thicker beams, which will be far more difficult to carry and install. If the space between two trees is too large, you can include posts, thereby reducing the gap to be bridged. Even if you have, for example, three trees in a row, you won't have the same creative leeway afforded by three trees arranged in an equilateral triangle; posts may be an additional help in such cases, too.

2.2
Choosing a tree

The tree you choose will become the focus and heart of your project, so it is important to take good care of it. Ultimately the tree holds the future of your treehouse.

As a rule, it is easier to build a treehouse with several trees, since it leaves you more room to maneuver with your design. You may have one tree, multiple trees, or no trees, but for simplicity, the text that follows is based on just one. Now let's choose a suitable tree.

The following information will help you determine the difference between a healthy tree and a weak one, and to better understand the tree and its needs. You will discover the dangers of placing additional strain on an already weakened tree, thereby risking potential damage. Care at this point will enable you to enjoy your treehouse for many years to come, and the tree will continue to grow as it wants (and as if you had never come along). Examine the tree you are sizing up as a candidate and ask the following questions:

- What species of tree is it?

- What condition is it in?

- How thick is its trunk?

- Are there birds' nests or squirrels' dreys in the tree? Are they occupied or are there even some eggs or young present? Please leave an inhabited tree alone; you don't want to drive anyone out of their home.

Check the list opposite for information on the suitability of different species for treehouse building. There are also lots of good books on tree identification and health to make your work easier, and at the back of this book you will find recommended further reading to help with your choice. Apps such as *iNaturalist* and *PlantNet* can be very useful when identifying a tree.

In general, deciduous trees are more suitable than evergreens for supporting treehouses, because they tend to live longer and are better at compartmentalization (healing their wounds). But, as you will see from the list, some evergreens are very acceptable options too.

Walk around the tree, use a ladder to climb it, and inspect it thoroughly before selecting it for the treehouse. Check its bark and branches, look out for cracks or hollows in the trunk, and locate any rotten or damp spots, or other anomalies. Is the crown large and luxuriant or has it undergone pollarding or radical pruning at some point? Does it stand at an obvious or strange angle? Does it have a fork? If so, check if the fork is U-shaped or V-shaped (see opposite); if V-shaped, it should have grown cleanly without forming a furrow, which may indicate a bark inclusion (bark growing into the tree). Such a junction may be detrimental to the fork's stability and may be a breaking point in high winds, for example.

Lots of dead branches in the crown can indicate disease. On deciduous trees, this is much easier to see in the summer, when the absence of leaves on dead limbs makes them stand out. Fractures and bark damage are reliable indicators of dead wood and/or storm damage, regardless of the season. If the tree is an oak, it might be at risk from the oak processionary moth. Check the tree for infestation; if there are silvery, shiny nests present, call an expert to get rid of the caterpillars. The bristles of this insect can cause severe allergic reactions in humans, and the caterpillar can strip the entire tree of greenery, causing lasting damage.

If you are concerned that the tree has any of the problems listed above, we advise you to find another tree or to build your treehouse with posts. If in doubt, consult an arborist (tree surgeon) to determine whether what you have discovered is an obstacle to the project. You can find tree experts on the American Society of Consulting Arborists website in the United States (www.asca-consultants.org) or the Arboricultural

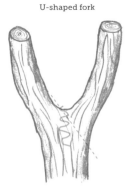
U-shaped fork

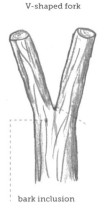
V-shaped fork

bark inclusion

The list below shows which species are generally suitable for a treehouse. You can also use it to compare species (but note that it is subject to natural variability). With species toward the bottom of the scale, such as willow and aspen, the tree requires very careful inspection before you build your treehouse in it. Species further up the scale, from beech to fir, are fine in theory as supporting trees. An important factor in the suitability of a tree for treehouse-building is how that particular species reacts to any injury it has suffered, and, specifically, its capacity for compartmentalization (see page 30).

Association website in the United Kingdom (www.trees. org.uk), along with all sorts of help and advice. Visual examination by amateurs may be reassuring and in some cases will suffice, but it cannot replace thorough inspection by a professional.

SIGNS OF A SUITABLE TREE

- Upright, healthy structure

- Large, luxuriant crown

- U-shaped fork

- V-shaped fork with no bark inclusion, i.e. angle overgrown with bark

- Plenty of branches with leaves on each twig (or buds in winter)

SIGNS OF A WEAKENED TREE

- Cracks in trunk or branches

- Hollows in trunk or branches

- Permanently damp spots

- Heavily pruned crown

- V-shaped fork with bark inclusion

- Entire tree is standing at a noticeable angle

- Lots of dead branches

- Numerous breaks and fractures that haven't healed

- Compacted soil around the tree

- Exposed roots

SUITABILITY FOR TREEHOUSE-BUILDING

Beech/copper beech
Hornbeam/whitebeam
Oak
Lime/linden
Larch
Maple
Pine
Ash
Plane
Chestnut
Robinia
Douglas fir
Walnut
Birch
Elm
Alder
Cherry
Cedar
Pear
Spruce
Poplar/black poplar
Horse chestnut
Aspen
Willow

*Source:
Vitus Wahlländer,
BA dissertation, 2015*

  Children can become actively involved from the beginning. Spark their interest with age-appropriate books from the Sources section (page 170), whether a storybook or an interesting reference book. Let them loose on a tree identification guide to pick out a good tree that they can measure and, depending on their ability, climb. Get them involved in identifying the tree and sketching your dream treehouse or theirs, or both.

2.3
Taking care of the tree

First, let's retrace our steps and take a look in greater detail at our tree in relation to a key property of this fascinating living thing: compartmentalization, or the power to seal off wounds.

Self-healing plays an important role in your treehouse build. There are of course infinitely more fascinating facts to recount about trees than this one aspect (see Sources, page 168), but let's concentrate on the essentials so that you can get started.

Trees have been growing and adapting to environmental conditions on our planet for millions of years. Over this time they have developed a range of strategies to compete with other trees. Some grow quickly and have a short life before decay sets in; trees of this kind plow all their energy into speedy growth and are less interested in repelling putrefactive agents or establishing robust structures. They focus on developing as quickly as possible to spread their seed. Such species include the willow, spruce, and poplar. Other trees grow more slowly and expend more energy on repelling rot. They form long-lasting structures and are the type of tree that you should be looking for. Trees in this category include oaks, beeches, lime trees, and larches.

You injure a tree every time you drill into it to mount a load-bearing element. Its vascular system (phloem and xylem), located directly beneath the bark alongside the cambium, will be interrupted by the drill hole. It's important to know that the tree is much better equipped to deal with such pinpoint interruptions than with wider obstructions, such as collars or cables. The supply of nutrients can flow around the point of interruption much more easily than it can where there are larger obstructions. The tree responds to the wound by placing the affected area under quarantine, compartmentalizing it and thereby preventing decay. Trees that are adept at this (those with a natural resistance to rot) are generally a better choice for a treehouse.

Trees that cannot compartmentalize well tend to develop decay along the length of wounds, for example just where the treehouse support is connected to the tree, which is of course not a good thing. Decay can also lead to the formation of cavities, which will reduce the lifespan of the treehouse.

Whatever the case, it is crucial to use as few bolts as possible to avoid causing unnecessary damage to the tree. The best bolts are the special tree attachment bolts used in this book, developed expressly for treehouse-building. Various characteristics of these bolts help the tree close the wound quickly, cleanly, and hermetically. The tree will adapt to the additional weight of the treehouse over time by forming reaction wood in the area under pressure beneath the bolts, integrating this growth into its system like an additional branch. The bolt might look brutal and intrusive, but its effect is the opposite: it is generally the best and gentlest method.

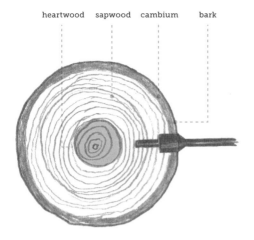

heartwood   sapwood   cambium   bark

It is during the building phase that you are most likely to damage the tree. The key thing to remember is that trees work on a much longer timescale than humans do, so something that stresses or injures a tree now might not register in terms of its health for years. When it does become apparent, it is often too late. Please take the following advice to heart to protect the tree, the most important element of the treehouse. As a treehouse-builder, you share responsibility for its well-being. Its health (closely followed by your own and that of your helpers) should always be of primary concern.

☞ Any wound is a potential point of entry for decay or pests, so it is better to drill a few large holes that you seal with TABs than several smaller, poorly sealed holes.

Tree health

PROTECT THE ROOTS

These hidden parts are extremely important for the tree's health. Consider what happens when you chop down a tree: many species will grow shoots from the tree stump and keep living, but if you take the felled tree and replant it, it will die very quickly because it is missing the roots that supply the water and nutrients essential for life, and where sugar and starch are stored for later use. Protect the roots and the tree is far more likely to survive the treehouse. Make sure you don't compact the earth around the tree too much or it will be more difficult for it to absorb nutrients, water, and oxygen. Before beginning construction, scatter a generous layer of woodchips and/or bark mulch around the base of the tree and any points of access to the trunk. Don't skimp: make this layer a good 4–6in (10–15cm) deep. In addition to distributing the pressure more evenly, you will be providing the soil with compostable material and helping the tree obtain extra nutrients. Place plywood planks across the mulch and/or woodchips to spread the weight of people and materials even more equally.

If, when digging out the foundations, you come across roots that are thicker than your thumb, don't just hack through them. Instead, dig around them, even if that involves removing soil with your hands. When you pour the concrete footings, first wrap the root in some foam or split a piece of piping lengthwise and lay it around the root. This allows it to continue growing and supplying the tree with nutrients.

These are the most important considerations for the health of the roots of the tree. If you don't protect the roots, you will end up with a wonderful treehouse in a stressed tree. In a worst-case scenario, it could result in the death of the tree or at least a long period of recovery.

WRAP THE BARK

The xylem, cambium, and phloem layers constitute the tree's life insurance. This system connects every root with every leaf and all the trunk tissue in between. If this connection is compromised, the development of the tree will be set back, which means that you must subject the tree to as few drill holes as possible. Less is more where tree health is concerned. When you install the structure, make sure that you don't injure the bark in the process; wrap the trunk and/or branches with, for example, thick fabric to protect the bark from damage by tools or building materials.

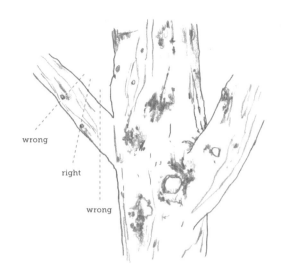

☞ Building a treehouse without bolts—for example, by attaching it with a clamp around the trunk or by laying load-bearing beams in the forks of branches (with the intention of not damaging it)—generally backfires. A clamp will constrict the tree over time and the beam in the fork of the branch will rub away the bark. Both will do considerable damage to the tree and make it vulnerable to rot and pests. Properly installed TABs with additional, well-situated hanging points using broad loop straps are always preferable.

wrong

right

wrong

REMOVE AS FEW BRANCHES AS POSSIBLE

Leaves are the nutrient producers. Every time you remove a branch, you also remove a source of nutrition. You will be hanging a considerable weight from the tree, causing damage to its bark, and cutting off a few branches, so the tree is going to need all the energy it can produce to reinforce injured areas, fight rot, and boost its ability to carry this new and unexpected weight in its crown. Use the correct cutting technique if you must remove branches (see illustration above): the cut face should be as small as possible for the tree to grow back over it as swiftly as it can. The cut should be made just above the branch ring, which will allow the tree to deal most effectively with the wound. Larger branches should be taken away in sections rather than cut off all at once. Make the first cut about 16in (40cm) from where you want to make the final one, then saw off the remaining stump at the branch ring; this will prevent the branch from breaking in an uncontrolled manner and causing damage to the tree.

LEAVE ROOM FOR THE TREE TO MOVE AND GROW

Trees sway in the wind and grow year after year, producing new growth rings annually and expanding in every direction. Make sure you leave the tree enough room for expansion. The higher you build, the greater the movement around the treehouse in the wind. Leave a gap of about 4in (10cm) between load-bearing beams and the tree, and at least 8in (20cm) clearance around the roof (the more room, the better). If the tree grows to reach the treehouse one day, you should be able to adapt the structure appropriately to accommodate such growth. Otherwise, the tree will slowly impair the stability of the structure by pushing it apart. Alternatively, the treehouse might damage the tree, but it is likely that both of these things will happen.

Are you happy with the tree and desperate to get started? We hear you. As you can see, the tree will end up making quite a few decisions for you; if you pay close attention, the tree will demonstrate how it can best support the treehouse, ensuring that the tree itself stays healthy over the long term with the structure in place. You will avoid many mistakes from the start by listening to the tree and designing your treehouse to suit it.

2.4
Positioning the treehouse

We chose a walnut tree with three trunks, around 80 years old, and about 40ft (12m) tall. It has a beautiful view over the yard and house, and of the surrounding fields and meadows beyond the property boundary.

There are two V-shaped forks about 3ft (1m) from the ground, so we must be careful. To make sure the tree is not subjected to unnecessary strain, we decided to use additional posts for our structure.

When deciding on a location for your treehouse, climb the tree, by ladder if necessary. Measure the distance between the branches and/or the trunks in which you intend to build the treehouse, along with the distance between the ground and the large branches, and the diameter(s) of the trunk(s). It doesn't have to be exact; it's more a matter of getting a better sense of the spatial relationships up in the tree. Have a look at how much clearance there is above, and which branches (as few as possible!) might have to be cut. As mentioned, remember to use the correct cutting technique so that the tree does not suffer unnecessary damage. Inspect it from all sides and factor in enough time for this part of the process. The ultimate goal is to find the perfect location for the treehouse. This may involve sacrificing one or two items on your wish list, but other possibilities might open up instead: the enormous bathtub might have to give way to a cozy reading corner, the spiral staircase may become a ladder leading up to a hatch in the floor, etc.

If you have several trees, mark out the distances between them on a horizontal plan. Label these with the most important dimensions, such as the diameters of the trees and the location and elevation from the ground of potentially intrusive branches. Check if the trees stand at an angle and make a note of this, including the direction and angle at which they lean, or you may end up running out of space between the trees further up.

Sketch the tree, ideally from all sides and from above. You will notice how you are becoming increasingly familiar with the tree, and how much easier it becomes to visualize the shape of the treehouse. Make copies of your tree diagram and sketch different versions of the treehouse, trying out and rejecting ideas before arriving at a definitive plan. You might want to pick up some inspiration from our website (www.baumbaron.de), where you will find some of the treehouses we have built, or take a look in Sources (pages 168–71).

Ask yourself a few questions and double-check the answers: Where can beams be hung? Is the trunk thick enough for a TAB? It should have a diameter of at least 16in (40cm). Do you want to build the treehouse as high up as possible? Keep in mind that, given the substructure, platform, walls, and roof truss, it will be pretty high already, so don't install the load-bearing beam too high or you risk leaving no space for the rest of the treehouse. More tips on how to proceed are detailed in "Measuring" on page 38.

> ☞ As a key rule, the lower the treehouse is attached to the tree, the bigger it can be.

USEFUL QUESTIONS TO CONSIDER WHEN POSITIONING THE TREEHOUSE

- Exactly where should the treehouse be located?

- What is the best position for the entrance and access route/ladder?

- At what height is there a particularly attractive view (perhaps the mountains, a local landmark/view, the sea, the sunset)?

- What direction should the balcony face, if you're adding one?

- Which side gets the sun?

- Which direction do the wind and weather generally come from and how exposed will the treehouse be to the elements?

- Is it possible to use tree attachment bolts?

- Is there somewhere to hang the treehouse?

- Is it possible to use post supports if required?

USEFUL QUESTIONS TO CONSIDER WHEN DESIGNING THE TREEHOUSE

- What is its primary use (kids' play house, bedroom, yoga room, sauna, office, craft or art room, or something else entirely)?

- Who will use it most (children, adults, grandparents, friends, guests, dogs, cats)?

- What's the maximum number of people it should be able to accommodate?

- What facilities should it have (sofa, bed, table, shower, and toilet)?

- Should it be a treehouse for all seasons?

Some of the answers to these questions will determine other factors, such as the planned use and consequent size of the treehouse. If your heart is set on having two double beds, a shower and toilet, plus a large table with chairs, it will be so big that you really shouldn't build it too high. An important consideration in determining the size of the treehouse will be the horizontal wind load, since the walls will act like a sail and encourage the tree to rock; the closer it is built to the ground, the lower the wind speed and the resulting lever action.

For more information about treehouse statics, see the section "Build Treehouse" at www.thetreehouse.shop.

FACTORS TO CONSIDER WHEN DESIGNING YOUR OWN TREEHOUSE

Match the *minimum ceiling height* to the intended users of the treehouse. This should be at least 5ft (1.5m) for children and at least 6ft (1.8m) for adults, except in a sleeping loft, where about 3ft (1m) should suffice—the key factor is the user's ability to sit upright. (Keep in mind that these figures are lower than the recommended ceiling heights for standard permanent dwellings.)

Plan in the eaves from the outset to ensure a sufficient gap between the treehouse and the tree; there must be at least 8in (20cm), and the more space, the better. Remember that strong winds will make the tree sway, and with insufficient clearance, damage could soon occur both to the tree and the treehouse.

When determining the *size of the platform*, remember that there should be space not just for the treehouse but also probably for a balcony and a walkway. The balcony should be at least 3ft (1m) wide and ideally more. Allow at least 24in (60cm) all around the treehouse for a walkway; this will make it easy to negotiate.

The *floor plan* of your treehouse should allow space for the furniture and so on that you will want to put in later, so remember to accommodate the dimensions of the furnishings: bed, table, sofa.

Research the *dimensions of certain materials* and components that you might wish to use; corrugated (box-profile) sheeting for covering the roof, for example, is available from home-improvement (DIY) stores as panels. If you plan the roof to match the sizes of these, you can reduce the cutting required and save on effort and outlay. Insulation panels are of a standardized width (4ft/1.2m in the USA and UK) that you can incorporate into planning the walls.

Avoid using weighty *materials*, such as stone slabs, steel parts, or large amounts of heavy wood such as oak.

Planning and sizing load-bearing beams

When figuring out the dimensions of the load-bearing beam for the substructure, remember the following rule of thumb: *beam length ÷ 20 = minimum beam width* (see diagram below). If in doubt, thicker is better! So, if the beam is 13ft (4m) long, it should be at least 8in (20cm) wide. *(Beam length 13ft/4m ÷ 20 = beam width 8in/20cm.)* If several beams are placed side by side (e.g. in the platform) and the weight of the treehouse is distributed across these beams, the width of the individual beams can be ½–1in (1–2cm) less, if necessary.

Post supports should be no longer than 10ft (3m); this reduces the risk of them breaking in the middle.

If the beam extends further than its support, be careful that this cantilever is not too long should the protruding end be destined to bear weight at some point in the future. The illustration below shows by approximately how much the beam can oversail, measured by beam width; the wider the beam, the further it can protrude. (Figures based on larch with 93N/m² bending strength, 300kg point load, safety factor 2.5.)

Once you know what your treehouse will look like, where it will be located (and at what elevation), and which furnishings and fittings will be included, you can finally get started. The design and plan in front of you (ours or your own) will turn into your treehouse over the weeks to come. You will need the following to start with:

1. A stable *substructure*, to which the

2. *platform* will be attached. This will be covered with

3. *baseboards*, on which

4. the *walls* are mounted. You can then fit and seal

5. the *roof* on top of these. After that, you will need to install

6. *doors and windows* to make it cozy, fit

7. a *handrail* all around so that no one falls off, then fit

8. an *entrance ladder*.

9. You're still missing your interior decoration, so grab some pillows, open a book, make sure you have drinks and cookies, and you're done!

10. *Special features*, such as a firefighter's pole and a climbing net, are the cherries on your treehouse cake.

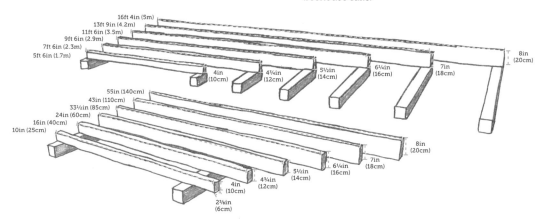

Choosing a thicker beam has a far less significant effect on any potential cantilever than choosing a wider beam.

☞ Treehouses are lightweight structures! Remember that the higher and/or larger the structure, the greater the demands in terms of time, budget, and workforce. Beams, boards, walls, windows, doors, roof parts—every item, right down to the last tiny screw—will have to be carried up the tree at some point, so think about how you will do this, which equipment and tools will be required, and how many assistants you will need. How high will the ladder end up, and at what height will future treehouse-dwellers still feel safe?

It's now time to turn our attention to the treehouse foundations. After you've chosen a healthy tree, the next key element of the build is a stable substructure, and this demands the utmost precision. The lifespan of your treehouse will depend on it. Load-bearing beams are not as easy to replace as the boards for the platform, for example, so make sure you allow yourself enough time and space to work on the substructure. Remember that it's better to check your design and measurements three times too often than once too few.

3

Building the Substructure

3.1
Substructure with larch posts

If you want to build without posts as supports, measure your tree carefully then follow up with sections 3.2 and/or 3.3, since the first load-bearing beams will ultimately have to hang from or lie on top of something. You will find more information in section 3.8.

If you have one or more trees and intend to work with support posts, start by measuring, attaching your tree attachment bolt(s), and hanging your loop strap. The tree should dictate the height at which your treehouse is built; you can adapt the height of the support posts later. Make sure no large roots run under the potential location of each post; make some careful test excavations first to avoid problems later when digging the holes for the footings. The closer to the tree you dig, the more likely you are to encounter a large root.

Once you have determined the location and elevation of your treehouse, you can get started. Your goal today is to identify the exact point on the tree to place the first load-bearing beam of your substructure and install it there.

  Children can enjoy lots of input at this stage by helping with measuring, marking out, digging foundations, and doing prep work. They will have plenty of opportunity to climb the tree and lots of time for their own projects (see suggestions in Sources, pages 168–71).

Measuring

One challenge when building a treehouse is to integrate its geometrical shape into surroundings that have grown organically. A tree is not that easy to measure without professional technical instruments. The method explained on pages 39–40 is just one of several possible approaches. Depending on your individual situation, one of these might prove simpler and more productive, so do some research before starting.

What to do on site

First, protect the roots by scattering woodchips or bark mulch to a depth of at least 4–6in (10–15cm) all around the tree; spread these out to reach as far from the trunk as the crown of the tree itself does. To protect the bark from mishaps, you might choose to wrap it in thick fabric, but make sure you remove this if you are unable to work on the treehouse for a while, especially if it rains during that time.

1

To make it easier for you to establish the exact position of your treehouse, screw a board of the same length as the load-bearing beam to the tree at the desired height (in our case, 2.48m/8ft 2in) or attach it with a lashing strap. This board will be removed later. Use a level (spirit level) to make sure it is horizontal.

This board now forms your provisional reference point and represents the load-bearing beam. Using it to work from, you can measure the precise location of the substructure, platform, and treehouse. Doing this will allow you to establish whether there is enough room for everything you intend to build up there.

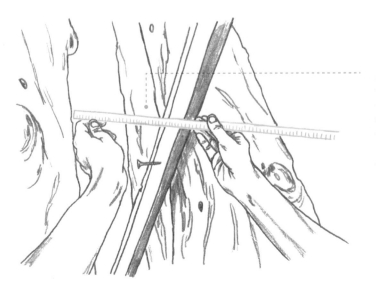

2

You must also make sure there is sufficient room for the load-bearing beam at the location it will later occupy. Leave clearance of 4in (10cm) between the load-bearing beam and the tree so that the tree can continue to grow and move.

3

Depending on the design of your substructure, keep in mind that the tree attachment bolt must be installed some way below the top edge of your baseboards, so make sure that it is possible to drill a hole and install the bolt in a suitable location.

1in (2.5cm)
4¾in (12cm)
4¼in (11cm)
1⅜in (3.5cm)

In our case, this assembly comprised:

- the bracket (its upper edge just over 1⅜in/3.5cm above the axis of the bolt)

- a load-bearing beam 4¼in (11cm) wide

- a platform 4¾in (12cm) thick and

- the 1in-thick (2.5cm) baseboards.

Measure a total of 11⅜in (29cm) down from the top side of your baseboards to the point where you should drill a hole.

4

If you want to suspend your load-bearing beam, make sure it is possible in the chosen location by establishing whether there is a suitable fork in the main trunk above the beam from which the loop strap can be securely suspended, and that the cable will not get in the way of the structure at a later point. The loop strap should not simply be suspended from a branch; instead, it should always be attached to the main trunk or a division of the trunk. Only use branches growing out of the fork in the trunk to prevent slippage. See illustration and section 3.3.

After you have finished measuring, fit the tree attachment bolt, install the loop strap, and dig some foundations. We describe all three options here (but your design might not involve them all, of course).

3.2
Using a tree attachment bolt

The tree attachment bolt is the load-bearing connection between your treehouse and the tree, and therefore the most important element in the structure after the tree itself. It is intended to act as an additional branch, securely bearing the weight of your treehouse.

You can't afford to make any mistakes, so measure twice (or several times) and double-check. You will have only one shot at this. But don't worry, if you are well prepared and follow our instructions, you will get it right!

For our treehouse, we used the GTS Allstar tree attachment bolt. This is a refinement of the Garnier Limb, named after its inventor Michael Garnier, a global pioneer of treehouse-building, who runs the Out 'n' About Treehouse Resort in Oregon. The GTS Allstar differs from the original design of the Garnier Limb in that it has been manufactured to be significantly more solid in structure. Various design details have been adapted to optimize wound closure and load-bearing properties in the tree, which will then be able to bear the additional load easily (as long as it is healthy and thriving and the bolt has been installed correctly). As mentioned on page 30, the tree will, over time, integrate the bolt into its system like an additional branch through the formation of reaction wood.

☞ The GTS Allstar tree attachment bolt is available in metric sizes. TABs by other manufacturers are available in both metric and imperial sizes; see page 171 for suppliers.

The GTS Allstar tree attachment bolt is available in metric sizes. TABs by other manufacturers are available in both metric and imperial sizes; see page 171 for suppliers.

TOOLS

- Basic equipment (see page 22)
- Powerful cordless drill (at least 70Nm torque, 22V 5.2Ah battery)
- Auger bit (1⅜in/36mm)
- Forstner bit (3in/74mm) with 1⅜in (36mm) shank
- Ratchet wrench plus 1⅞in (46mm) socket
- Robust steel tube as a cheater bar for more leverage (optional)
- Level (spirit level), surveyor's level, or water level
- Rubber mallet
- Disinfectant
- Clean cloth
- Climbing gear for safety

You can rent the auger bit, Forstner bit, and ratchet from a hardware store or tool-rental center, so you don't need to spend large sums on them only to have them lying around and gathering dust once the project is complete. A corded power drill is not right for this stage of the project; unlike a cordless drill, it does not stop as soon as you let go of the trigger, which poses a serious hazard for your wrists!

MATERIALS

- GTS Allstar tree attachment bolt plus nut, and a bracket
- ½x4in (10x100mm) hex wood screws to mount the bracket

What to do on site

1

Make sure you have everything handy. The less time between drilling the hole and screwing in the bolt, the better it will be for the tree; the less resin/sap flowing into the drill hole, the easier it is to screw in the bolt. First, identify the precise point on the tree trunk at which you are going to drill the hole for the tree attachment bolt (TAB) by measuring the distance between the top edge of the load-bearing beam and the center of the bolt.

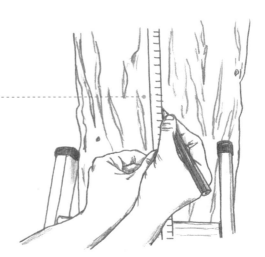

2

Measure the desired elevation of the load-bearing beams above the ground and mark it clearly on the tree.

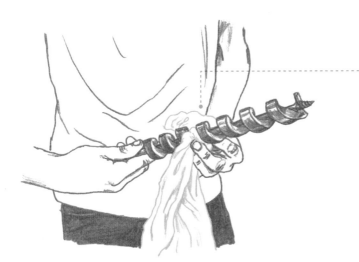

3

Just before drilling, carefully clean and disinfect the drill bit to prevent fungal spores or other contaminants from entering the hole. Fit the TAB immediately after drilling to similarly prevent contamination.

4

Once you are certain that you have the right spot, prepare to drill a hole exactly 7¼in (18.5cm) deep toward the center of the trunk. Use a small piece of duct tape to mark off this depth on the auger bit so you will always know how deep the bit has gone. Place a small level (spirit level) directly on the auger bit to make sure it is horizontal. The bolt should be as perpendicular to the beam as possible so that the bracket can be seated and installed correctly.

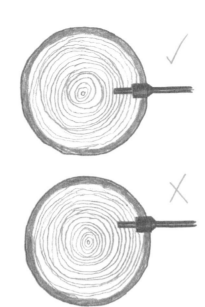

5

Choose the strongest member of the team to take charge of the drill, employing the additional side handle (see left arm in image) to guide the drill bit (which might otherwise tilt) without twisting their (or your) wrist. Make sure they have a secure footing and are attached safely with a climbing harness and a rope if working on a ladder.

Remember to drill horizontally and at a right angle to the load-bearing beam you are going to install. Withdraw the drill bit several times and clear it of drilling chips. Take this opportunity to check the depth of the hole.

⚠ Unusually soft or heavily stained drilling chips are a sign of decay in the tree, in which case you can't use a tree attachment bolt as a support at this location because there is no guarantee that it can bear the weight safely. The tree must be inspected closely by an expert before you continue with your build.

6

Once you have reached a depth of 7¼in (18.5cm), switch to the Forstner bit and drill until the larger hole is at least 2½in (6.5cm) deep. Measure this from the cambium, i.e. the point where the dark part of the bark transitions to a slightly lighter layer. The key aim here is that the thick part of the bolt can be screwed in as far as the thicker conical flange.

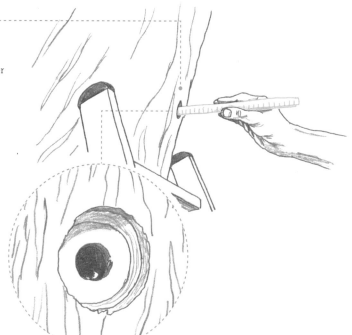

7

To provide an additional seal against fungal spores in the drill hole and to seat the TAB more securely from the outset, coat the end of the coarse thread and the surface of the cylindrical section of the bolt with polyurethane glue. If you don't have any glue handy, just screw the bolt in with no coating. Use a heavy rubber mallet to hammer the TAB in a little, to keep it from falling out. Screw it in manually a few turns and thread the nut on to the fine thread at the end of the bolt if you have not already done this.

☞ After drilling the hole, if you discover that you have made a mistake in your measurements and positioned the bolt a little too low, place a wooden board of a suitable thickness between the support bracket and the load-bearing beam to fill the gap. Make sure you glue the board on so that it doesn't slip out of position over time. If the bolt is too high, place something of an appropriate thickness under the other end of the load-bearing beam. If the position of the bolt is completely wrong, do not leave the drill hole open to the elements or the tree will have an open wound that provides easy access for pests and decay. If in doubt, tighten the bolt anyway and, if necessary, cut off the protruding part with an angle grinder.

8

Use the ratchet to tighten the TAB until it is firmly seated. Make sure the bolt stays horizontal as you tighten it. If required, get more leverage with a robust steel tube slid over the handle of the ratchet as an extension "cheater bar." As soon as the back of the thicker center section of the bolt reaches the tree, it will become noticeably more difficult to tighten and you will know that it is properly seated. There is sometimes a creaking sound as you do this because the thicker part of the bolt creates vibrations in the tree through friction with the wood. Use caution with softer woods, such as spruce: you must be careful not to overtighten the bolt.

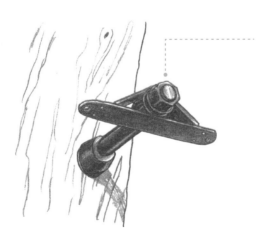

9

Switch the ratchet to reverse and loosen the nut. Slide on the bracket and tighten up the nut again. The load-bearing beam can now be attached to the bracket. The bracket shown here points downward because of gravity. You must turn it around before placing the load-bearing beam on top.

10

If you have several trees, you can also install several bolts as supports (see 3.8). Use a homemade water level (a transparent length of tubing filled with water) or a surveyor's level to make sure that the bolts are at exactly the same height for the platform to be level. If you use a water level, make sure no air bubbles are left in the tubing or your measurements will be wrong; the water will always be at exactly the same level at both ends of the tube if you remove all the bubbles. A water level is a cheap but highly reliable and precise measuring instrument.

3.3
Hanging a loop strap

Along with a tree attachment bolt, you can use a steel cable to hang your treehouse from the tree. This offers an elegant solution while causing minimal damage, and is particularly good for temporary installations, or in places where the insertion of a tree attachment bolt is impossible.

The advantages of this substructure method include causing no harm to the tree, which can move freely; low cost; and a large load-bearing capacity (anything up to 4–8 tons). Disadvantages include the fact that the position of your platform may be dictated by the location of the cable; the cable may get in the way as you move around the treehouse; and the structure will be susceptible to vibrations during high winds. Make sure to locate a suspended structure as low as possible (the higher you hang it, the greater the movement by wind) because, if the cable, branch, or bough fails at any point, it may happen abruptly. This is in stark contrast to the use of a tree attachment bolt, where failure would become obvious as the bolt slowly bent out of shape. We used loop straps to facilitate the long cantilever of our load-bearing beam, and of course to offer you alternative means of building.

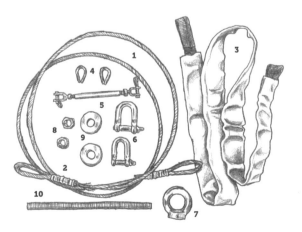

What to do on site

Ideally, place your loop strap around the main trunk to hang the load-bearing beam; alternatively, select one side of a forked trunk, which should be as thick as possible. Use branches as an anti-slip measure only. Make sure there is room for the tree to grow—the loop should be placed loosely around the trunk, not strangling it. To repeat: the higher the suspension point, the more wind movement the treehouse will be exposed to, so install your suspension mounting as low as possible. The final angle between the suspended load-bearing beam and the steel cable should always be between 45 and 90 degrees; this will hold the weight of your suspended structure well.

45–90°

1

Make sure the loop strap is lying flat to the trunk all the way around and is not twisted.

Measure the approximate distance between the suspension point and the load-bearing beam, following the path where the steel cable is going to run and first trimming away any intrusive branches and twigs if there is no other option. Remember the correct cutting technique here; see section 2.3.

☞ Check all parts of your suspension assembly for compatibility. This means that all the parts can be connected and that they have matching load-bearing capacities. If not, you could end up with a weak link in your suspension "chain." It is always better to use stainless steel, which lasts longer and does not rust.

2

Use the crimping tool to cut the steel cable to the desired length. Leave about 3ft (1m) of excess in addition to the distance you measured between the suspension point and the load-bearing beam; this will give you more leeway and you can pull on this end when you tension the cable later.

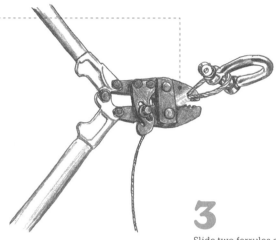

3

Slide two ferrules on to the steel cable. Wrap the cable around the thimble and thread the end back through the ferrules to create a tight loop from which the thimble cannot escape. Use the crimping tool to crimp each of the ferrules together three times (three times is a charm—making sure of this connection will enable the responsible treehouse-builder to sleep at night). Wrap the cut-off end with duct tape (or, for a more elegant solution, whip it very tightly with thin nylon thread so that the wire won't fray and injure people who are climbing past). Undo the shackle and use it to link the loop strap to the steel cable. Tighten the shackle firmly and you are done.

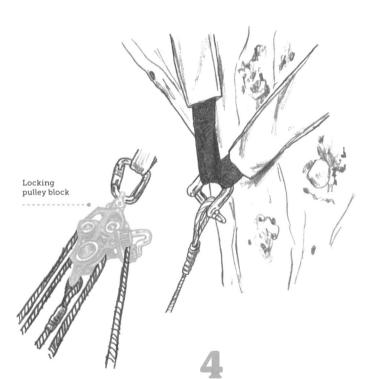

Locking pulley block

4

Install the temporary suspension assembly for the load-bearing beam so you can haul it up and keep it in position. The best thing to work with here is a locking pulley block, which will make your work a breeze by giving you a 3:1 mechanical advantage, enabling you to lift the load-bearing beam into its exact position. If you don't have access to a pulley block, a strong rope passed over a suitable pulley attached to the tree will do the job.

5

Wrap the loop strap around the load-bearing beam, then fasten the lower end of the pulley block cable/rope to it. You can of course fasten the rope directly to the load-bearing beam, but make sure it can't slip off; you might want to attach it securely with a small screw.

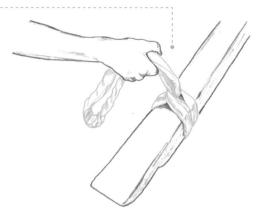

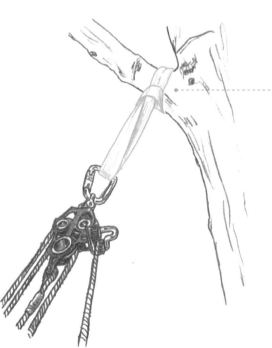

6

Sling a second loop strap around the trunk or a strong branch. Hang the upper block of the pulley (the one with the cam cleat that locks the rope) from it.

7

Attach the lower block to the loop strap on the load-bearing beam. Now haul the beam to the desired height.

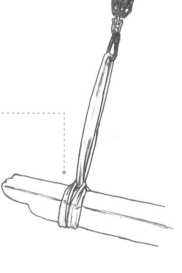

8

Push up the other end of the load-bearing beam so it sits on the bracket. Get one person to hold it in place while another secures the pulley block.

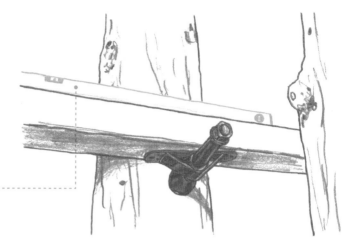

9

Both of you should work the load-bearing beam into position together. Use a level (spirit level) to make sure it is level, then temporarily fix the bracket to the load-bearing beam with two screws.

10

Drill a hole ⅝in (16mm) in diameter in the load-bearing beam to fit the M16 threaded rod, measuring 16in (40cm) in from the suspended beam end and drilling into the middle of the beam.

Angle grind the threaded rod to a suitable length (equal to the thickness of the beam plus washers and nuts), or hammer a suitable carriage bolt or hex bolt into the hole.

Of course, you can also drill the hole before you lift the beam. Just make sure the hole is positioned so that nothing obstructs the steel cable later.

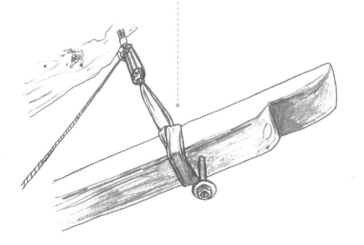

⚠ Caution: the sparks that fly up when using an angle grinder can leave unsightly marks on larch after a while, so cover your larch workpieces well if using an angle grinder anywhere nearby.

12

Thread the lower end of the steel cable through the upper end of the turnbuckle, running it through a thimble to protect it, and pull the cable tight.

13

Close up the cable loop you have created with two ferrules and tension the whole assembly with the turnbuckle until the load-bearing beam hangs horizontally.

11

Thread the ring nut on top and tighten it. You can tighten it more firmly by using a pipe wrench or a screwdriver inserted into the ring nut. Connect the ring nut to the shackle and the half-tightened turnbuckle. This will leave you with a bit of leeway for height adjustment later.

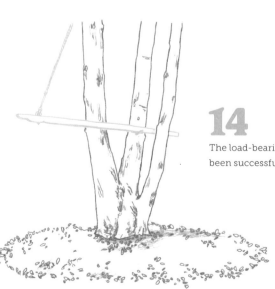

14

The load-bearing beam has been successfully suspended.

☞ In some states or countries, regulations stipulate that a tree loop strap be replaced after a certain number of years, regardless of its condition. Be sure to check the rules in your area.

3.4
Posts

If you'd like to reduce the strain on your tree, or if it is too delicate to bear the weight of a treehouse on its own, support posts are the best option.

Posts have a very high load-bearing capacity, enabling the use of heavy materials or fixtures and fittings (such as a bathtub) in your treehouse. The advantages of using posts include making it easier to figure out the structural parameters of your project, and great stability. When you are digging out foundations, however, look out for roots, which can be easily damaged.

The simplest and most stable support method is to prop up your treehouse with larch posts, as described here. If you plan to support your platform with angled robinia logs, however, continue working from section 3.6. If you have no trees to work with, head to section 3.7, where the method described here is explained again. In that case you will need four posts rather than two for your treehouse to have a secure footing.

TOOLS

- Basic equipment (see page 22)
- Miter saw
- Plummet/plumb bob
- Long level (spirit level), surveyor's level, or water level
- Line marker spray
- Spade, shovel, pickaxe (optional), small scoop, trowel
- Robust mortar tub or large bucket for mixing
- Drill with paddle mixer attachment

MATERIALS

- Larch beams, 4×4in (11×11cm)
- Larch joists, 2×4in (6×11cm)
- Fast-setting or standard concrete
- Post support, ideally height-adjustable
- Joist hanger, 4¼×4¼in (110×110mm)
- Yardstick or board to extend the level (spirit level) (optional)
- Stainless-steel screws:
  - #12×4in (6×100mm)
  - #12×5½in (6×140mm)
- Galvanized screws:
  - #12×8⅝in (6×220mm)
  - #12×9½in (6×240mm)
- M6 carriage bolts: 5½in (140mm)
- Express anchor

The substructure with larch posts will look like this when you have completed this section.

What to do in the workshop

1

Cut the beams and joists for the substructure to size, taking your dimension from page 6 of the construction plan. Mount the posts, including braces 1 and 2, and the cross member. Connect the beam with 8⅝in (220mm) screws, and the cleats with 5½in (140mm) screws. Drill a pilot hole with a ¼in (6mm) drill bit and screw in the screws as perpendicular as possible to the face of the wood. A little glue will also strengthen the joints. Mark the faces of the remaining lumber (timber) with their lengths for ease of identification later.

What to do on site

2

First, locate the positions of your footings on the ground. To do this, transfer two defined points up on the load-bearing beam to the ground using a plumb bob. Measure the distances on the ground and determine the position of the substructure and/or the footings. In the absence of a plumb bob, make one with a length of string and an eye bolt.

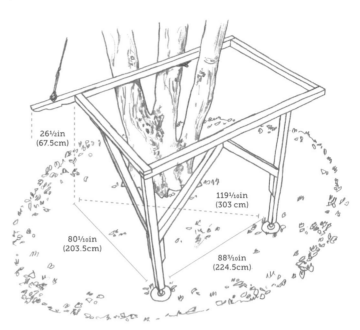

26½in
(67.5cm)

119¹⁄₁₀in
(303 cm)

80¹⁄₁₀in
(203.5cm)

88³⁄₁₀in
(224.5cm)

3

Measure 26½in (67.5cm) in from the end of the suspended load-bearing beam. Use the plumb bob to find the point on the ground beneath this and mark by fixing a long screw into the ground. Mark the distance to the next plumb bob point (88³⁄₁₀in/224.5cm) on the load-bearing beam and use the plumb bob to transfer this to the ground in the same way. Mark this point with a long screw too.

4

Connect the two points on the ground with a batten or piece of string. Strike a line 80¹⁄₁₀in (203.5cm) long at a right angle from each end of this line and mark these points with a long screw. The two newly created points must be 88³⁄₁₀in (224.5cm) apart. These are the center points for the footings for your substructure with larch posts, and it is here that you will dig later. Final check: the diagonals between the plumb bob points on the ground and the center points of the foundations must be 119¹⁄₁₀in (303cm) long.

5

Once you are certain that the positions of the footings are correct, mark them with a generous application of line marker spray.

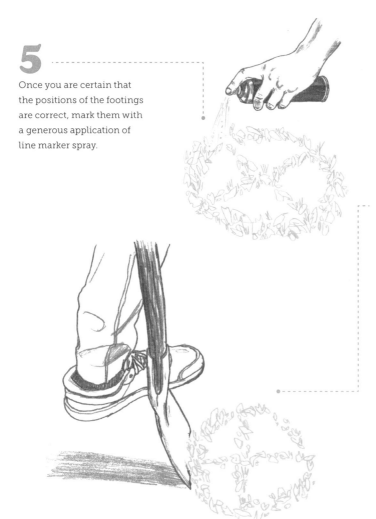

6

Begin digging and lifting the soil from the holes with a spade; the footings should be 12–16in (30–40cm) wide and 32in (80cm) deep. Switch to the shovel when you can get no further with the spade. A pickaxe will help if there are lots of stones. While digging, keep an eye out for the roots of surrounding trees. It's better to get your hands dirty and dig carefully around roots than to hack through them, especially if they are thicker than your thumb. When you pour the concrete foundations, first wrap the root with some plastic or surround it with some tubing that you have slit lengthwise. This will allow it to keep on growing and providing the tree with nutrients.

7

Mix the concrete with water in the mortar tub or bucket, stirring as directed by the manufacturer, or until the mixture has a consistency somewhere between that of pancake and cake batter. Pour the mixture into the holes and tamp it down with a piece of squared timber to make sure there are no air bubbles left. The top surface of the footings should be flush with the ground.

☞ In temperate climates foundations are considered frost-protected below a depth of 32in (80cm); the ground and the water inside it don't freeze below this depth and therefore don't expand during cold weather, which would lift the footing. Building regulations in most countries and states specify a minimum depth (to the underside of the foundation), so check the up-to-date rules in your area.

3.5
Cutting the posts

Once the footings have cured, it's time to get measuring.

You must now cut your posts to the correct length; the top edge of the cross members of your substructure (which will stand on the footings) will be at exactly the same height as the top edge of your load-bearing beam on the tree.

The best way to ensure this is to use a surveyor's level, which may be a laser or an optical device. Both are very expensive, but you can rent rather than buy them. Consult the instruction manual to learn how these devices work and how to operate them.

If you don't have access to either of these devices, work with a long level (spirit level) and a tape measure, or use a homemade water level (see page 45, step 10).

Two things you cannot do without are a large, free-standing ladder (stepladder) and some help. Stand the ladder next to the footing. One person should now lay the long level horizontally on the load-bearing beam, pointing toward the footing. If your level is not long enough, extend it by attaching a yardstick or a batten. Make sure that your extension level doesn't sag but stays straight. Take a batten or a board, place it vertically on the footing, and rest the level on it while measuring to keep it from wobbling.

Optical surveyor's level

Laser surveyor's level

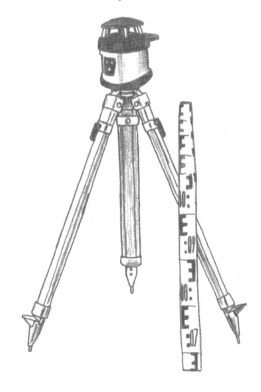

1

Measure the height of the level (spirit level) above each footing and note both these distances. This is how high your substructure must be. If the distances above each footing are different, the posts must also be cut to suitably different lengths so that everything ends up horizontal and the same height.

The approach is much the same when using the water level: one of you holds one end of the tubing against the load-bearing beam on the tree so that the surface of the water is flush with the top edge of the load-bearing beam, while the other end is held above the footing by a second person on the stepladder. Place a batten or board vertically on the footing and hold the water level against this while measuring to keep it from wobbling. Use a tape measure to measure the height of the water surface over each footing.

2

Let's turn to the prefabricated elements of the substructure. You must still deduct the height of the post anchors from the distances you have measured. The choice of post anchor is largely up to you; some must be set in concrete, while others are screwed to the finished footing. We recommend the latter: use an adjustable version of the most solid model you can find, like the one shown here, which has numerous attachment options. If you make a mistake in measuring or cutting, smaller errors can be resolved with an adjustable post anchor of this kind.

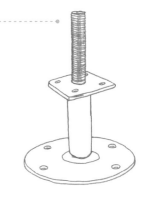

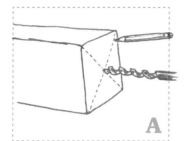

A

B

3

Once you have calculated and marked the final length of your posts, make sure the results are correct before making any cuts (measure twice, cut once). Ask a second person to double-check the measurements. If your post anchor has a thread to screw into the post, mark the center of the bottom face of each post and drill a suitable hole (A), making sure it is exactly aligned with the post so the post anchor will be perfectly seated. Smear a little glue inside the drill hole (B) then screw the post anchor into place until it is flush (C, D), using suitable screws. Finally, tighten the bolt (E, F).

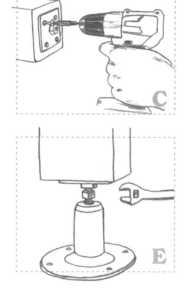

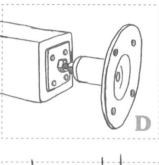

C

D

E

F

4

You can now erect the assembly with the help of your assistant(s). Arrange the prefabricated substructure on the footings and slide it into the correct position so that the clearance between the top of the structure and the load-bearing beam on the tree corresponds to the length of your connecting beam, which in our case was 198cm (78in). Make sure the substructure stands vertically.

5

Support the substructure with battens or boards on all sides and attach these with screw clamps or screws. Screw boards or battens to the bottom of the load-bearing beam at the points where the connecting beams will be attached (attach them with screw clamps if you want to avoid screw holes). This will help to keep the substructure in the right position and later provide support that will make it easier to attach the connecting beams.

6

Lay each connecting beam along the support boards and screw to the load-bearing beam at one end and the cross member of the substructure at the other. Installation dimensions are available on page 5 of the plan.

7

You can now remove the support boards. Apply glue to cleat 1 and attach the cleat to the connecting beam as described on page 7 of the plan, using 5½in (140mm) screws. Apply glue to the appropriate surfaces of brace 3 and position it in the cleat. If required, shift the substructure into position so that the brace is cleanly seated in both cleats before screwing everything together securely with 8⅝in (220mm) screws. You should also attach the joist hanger to the load-bearing beam to provide additional support for the connecting beam; this will make the connection more stable. The joist hanger is essential at this point because much of the treehouse weight will be centered here later.

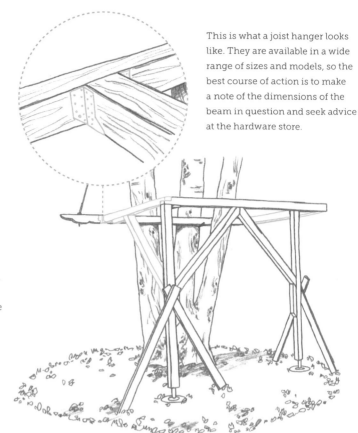

This is what a joist hanger looks like. They are available in a wide range of sizes and models, so the best course of action is to make a note of the dimensions of the beam in question and seek advice at the hardware store.

8

Now head to section 4.1 and work through this as far as step 15, then return to this section to mount brace 4. In this version of the structure, brace 4 provides a connection between the substructure and the platform, which is why you need to read part of the next section at this point.

Is the platform installed? Excellent. Now insert brace 4 into the remaining cleat, apply glue to the appropriate surfaces, and offer the lap up to the platform joist above. Make sure the post is absolutely vertical before screwing the brace securely into place.

9

If you first fix the brace in place with two 4in (100mm) screws, you can drill the hole for the carriage bolt later. The hole should be in the center of the lap joint. Push a 5½in (140mm) carriage bolt through, add the washer and nut, and tighten.

10

Job done. Your post anchors still need to be attached to the footings and the best way is with suitable express anchors. First make sure your uprights are exactly vertical; once they have been attached, you won't be able to move them. It is absolutely essential that the footings are entirely cured for this step.

Express anchor

A
Use a hammer drill and the appropriate drill bit to drill through the holes in the post anchor baseplate into the footing.

B
Use a hammer to knock each express anchor into the holes.

C
Tighten them with an impact screwdriver or wrench (spanner). Now turn to section 4.2 and continue boarding out the base.

3.6
Substructure with robinia logs

If you plan to build your treehouse with angled robinia supports, as we did, it's best to start by building scaffolding to the same height as your substructure; this will make it easier to get the angled posts into position.

You can build a robust frame from 2×2in (6×6cm) battens and/or boards that will also serve as a support for the beams of your substructure. This support should be located where the connecting beams will be installed later. See plan, page 11. For this step, it is essential to have a helper who has experience in using a chainsaw.

☞ Robinia (*Robinia pseudoacacia*; also known as false acacia or black locust) is almost the only wood that is durable enough to withstand being set into the ground or into concrete without rotting. It is extremely strong and hard, and is commonly available. Any other timber (except perhaps oak) would require a column footing to protect it when used in this way.

What to do on site

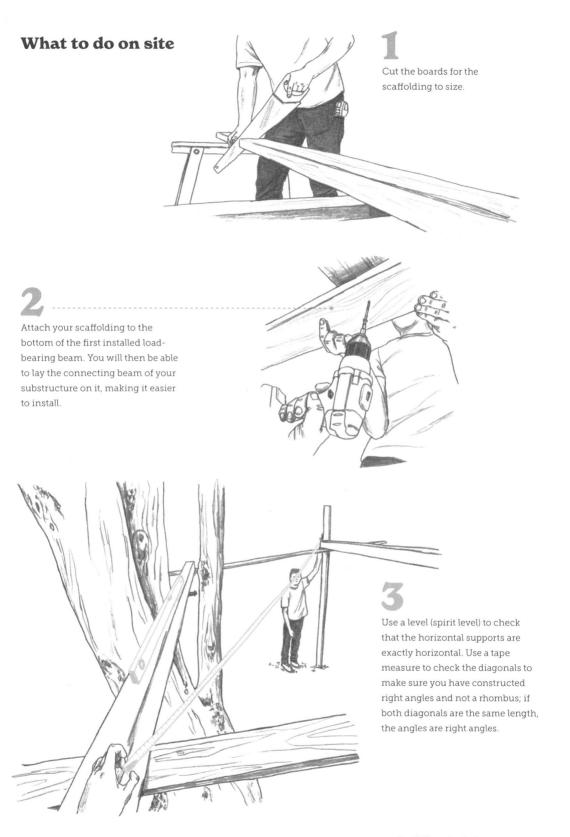

1

Cut the boards for the scaffolding to size.

2

Attach your scaffolding to the bottom of the first installed load-bearing beam. You will then be able to lay the connecting beam of your substructure on it, making it easier to install.

3

Use a level (spirit level) to check that the horizontal supports are exactly horizontal. Use a tape measure to check the diagonals to make sure you have constructed right angles and not a rhombus; if both diagonals are the same length, the angles are right angles.

4

If the lengths are different, correct the positioning of the supports until they are equal. Support the scaffolding at the front with vertical boards or battens and brace it to the sides as well. Your right-angled structure should now look like this.

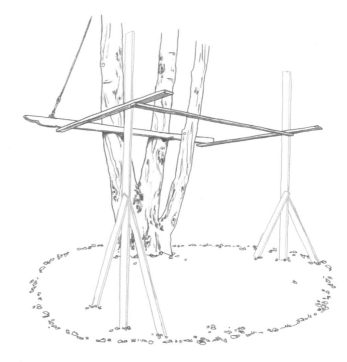

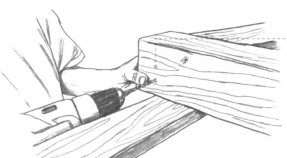

5

Offer up the cross member and connecting beam. You can identify the precise positions from the installation dimensions on page 11 of the plan. Drill a pilot hole first then screw everything together.

6

Drill at a slight angle since you are screwing into end grain here, i.e. in the same direction as the wood fibers run, to increase the solidity of your joint if the screw does not run entirely parallel to the grain. In this case (beams screwed together at right angles), select screws that are at least twice as long as the thickness of the beams you are screwing into. To be on the safe side, also use suitable joist hangers.

7

Measure the diagonals of the structure you have created so far in both directions to check that the beams of the substructure form right angles. Get on the ladder, figure out the precise lengths required for the robinia logs, and mark these on the logs. Don't forget to include in your calculations the fact that about 12–16in (30–40cm) of each robinia log will be sunk into the ground or concreted in.

Offer up the robinia logs to the top of the cross member; you can come inward about 8in (20cm) on each side. They should ultimately stand at an angle no greater than 15 degrees, otherwise the substructure will be difficult to stabilize.

5–15°   5–15°

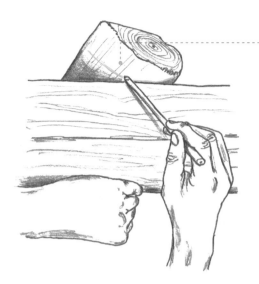

8

Mark where to cut to make the lap joint on the robinia log, using a pencil to draw two lines along the level of the cross members: one for the top edge of the cross member and one for the bottom edge. This lap joint will create a support for the cross member of the substructure while simultaneously providing a suitable surface when screwing the cross member to the robinia log.

9

At this point also mark the position of the robinia logs on the ground with line marker spray. First, spray a circle around the point, then a cross in the center of the circle. If you extend the lines of this cross beyond the circumference of the circle, you will be able to tell where the center of the hole is when your digging is at an advanced stage.

10

Use the chainsaw to lop off the end of the log and make the lap joint. Using the correct technique and ensuring that you are wearing the right protective gear (long pants/ trousers, boots, and hearing and eye protection) will remove the fear from this part of the process, but you must let someone with experience show you what to do, or do it for you. Safety first! Chainsaw lessons are available (for a reason) to show you how to use these tools safely.

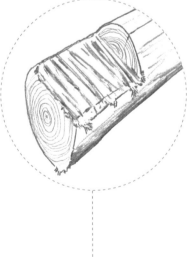

The lap joint should look something like this.

11

Use a spade to start lifting the turf and digging out the soil for the holes. You should dig out 4–8in (10–20cm) all around the posts, and the holes should be 32in (80cm) deep.

Switch to the shovel once you are unable to proceed further with the spade, using a pickaxe if there are lots of stones. When digging, keep an eye out for tree roots. Always dig around them carefully rather than hacking through them, especially if they are thicker than your thumb. Your tree needs its roots to live, and you need the tree as the future bearer of your treehouse—so always treat it with respect and care.

12

Insert the robinia logs into the holes and adjust them into position.

13

Drill two pilot holes in each lap and fix each robinia log in place with two wood screws. A film of glue on the cut face of the wood will protect it from damp and make the joint more secure. Drill a ½in (12mm) hole through the center of each lap and cross member.

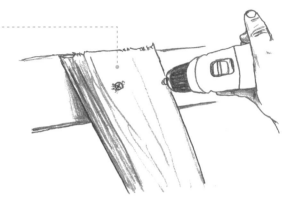

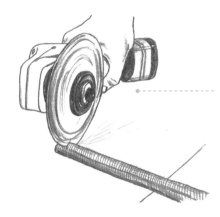

14

Angle grind an M12 threaded rod to a suitable length, which will be: *beam thickness + thickness of lap + washers and nuts* for both sides, or just take a suitable carriage bolt and/or hex screw and hammer it in place.

15

Thread the washer and nut on to the other end of the threaded rod and tighten securely.

☞ If you use fast-setting concrete for the foundations, you will be able to keep working that same day. With standard concrete, you may have to wait two or three days for it to cure, or there is a risk that the footings will crack and you will be back to square one. The dust created is harmful to your lungs and can damage and dry out your skin, so wear a dust mask and gloves.

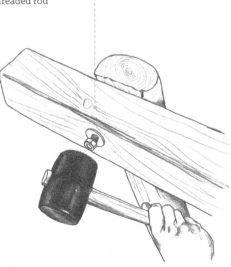

16

Mix the concrete with water in the mortar tub or bucket, stirring as directed by the manufacturer, or until the mixture has a consistency somewhere between that of pancake and cake batter.

Carefully pour the mixture into the holes, distributing it evenly around the robinia logs, and tamp it down with a piece of squared timber to make sure there are no air bubbles left.

17

The structure is now done! Crack open something to drink and celebrate your progress with your team. No one should go up on the platform or work on it until the concrete has cured, or the robinia logs could come loose in their foundations and the whole structure will no longer be on a secure footing.

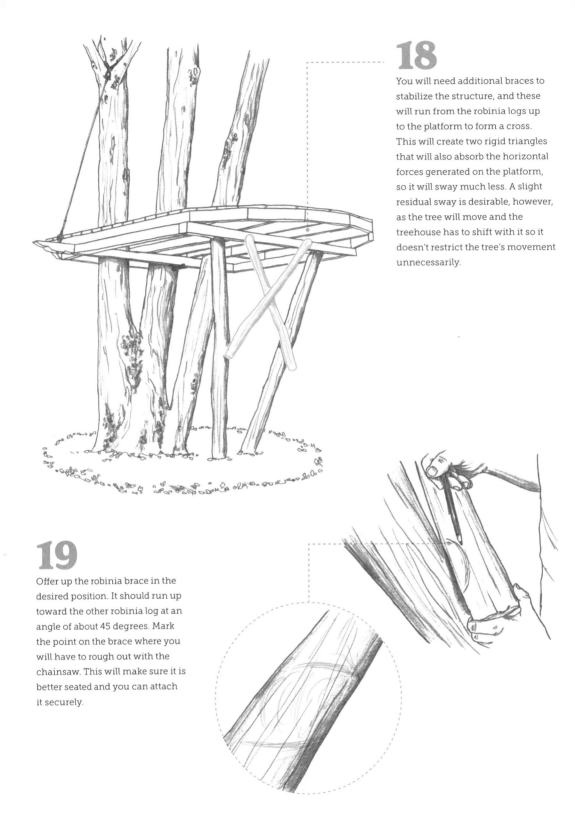

18

You will need additional braces to stabilize the structure, and these will run from the robinia logs up to the platform to form a cross. This will create two rigid triangles that will also absorb the horizontal forces generated on the platform, so it will sway much less. A slight residual sway is desirable, however, as the tree will move and the treehouse has to shift with it so it doesn't restrict the tree's movement unnecessarily.

19

Offer up the robinia brace in the desired position. It should run up toward the other robinia log at an angle of about 45 degrees. Mark the point on the brace where you will have to rough out with the chainsaw. This will make sure it is better seated and you can attach it securely.

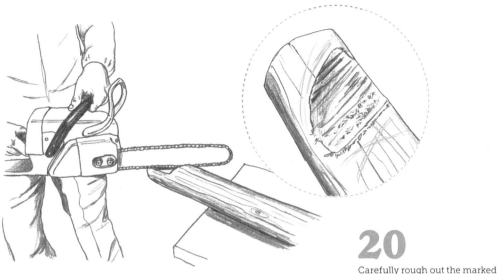

20

Carefully rough out the marked area with the chainsaw. As you proceed, constantly check the position, orientation, and depth of the area you are working on by offering up the brace to its intended position and checking to see if it is properly seated.

21

Once everything fits nicely, clamp the braces into position with screw clamps. Using a ½in (12mm) drill bit, drill a hole through the center of the brace and log, ideally with the exit hole also in the center.

22

Angle grind another M12 threaded
rod to a suitable length and thread
it through the robinia log and brace,
or hammer in a carriage bolt of a
suitable length. Mount the washer
and nut and tighten securely.

23

Is the lateral motion of your
platform still too great, even after
reinforcement with the additional
braces? In other words, does it feel
unstable or wobbly? You can also
install an additional treehouse
attachment bolt (TAB) with
a bracket to inhibit this sideways
movement. A suitable location
for this would be at a sufficiently
thick point on the tree trunk as far
away as possible from the first TAB
you installed. For our treehouse,
this position is shown in the
illustration.

    Now keep working on the
platform (see 4.1).

3.7
Substructure with no tree

A substructure with four support posts will allow you to put a treehouse wherever you want, even without a tree in sight.

You can build near trees, of course—you could even allow a tree to grow through your platform without it supporting the weight of part of the treehouse; the more greenery surrounding your little home away from home, the better. The structure and approach are similar to those described in section 3.4, the difference being that instead of a load-bearing beam on a tree, you have two additional posts with a cross member on top. These are joined to the other two posts with two connecting beams, and there are eight braces to make sure the whole structure is stable.

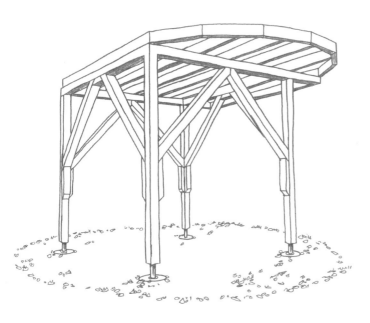

What to do in the workshop

1

Cut the beams and battens for the substructure to size according to the specifications on pages 14–17 of the plan. Completely assemble the framework on pages 14 and 15 of the plan in advance. The aim of this section is to construct a base to support the platform in four places, as illustrated right.

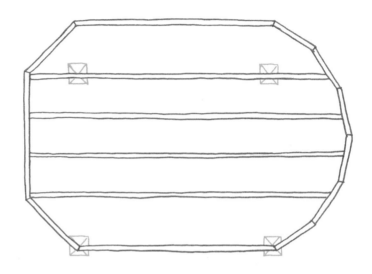

What to do on site

2

The footings are the first task. Having selected a beautiful location for your treehouse, make sure there is enough space on all sides for the whole structure, all the way up to the last gable crown. When choosing your footings, remember that the platform above will jut out beyond the foundations on three sides, so make sure it is possible to dig where you will have to do so.

3

Dig out the footings for the substructure at the intervals indicated in step 4, always measuring from the center of each footing to the next. Each hole should be 12–16in (30–40cm) wide and 32in (80cm) deep.

Now refer to section 3.4 for the steps to follow from digging and laying the footings to attaching the post anchors to their foundations. Once the footings have cured, next comes erecting your substructure. You will need a team of six for the following steps, or you could manage it with two people if you are strong and if you support your frame with battens and boards.

4

Stand the two prefabricated assemblies on the footings, ensuring their correct orientation: the two 45-degree mitered ends of the cross members must face each other. The two assemblies must be parallel; the footings will give you the approximate distance between them. The exact clearance between the two assemblies (i.e. the distance from the inner edge of one post to the inner edge of the other) must be 98½in (250cm), which corresponds to the length of connecting beams 2 and 3.

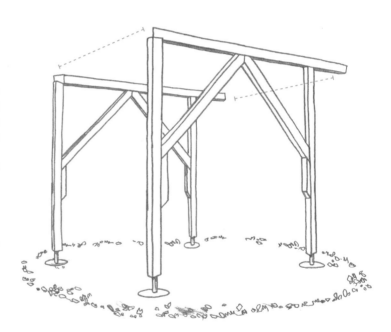

5

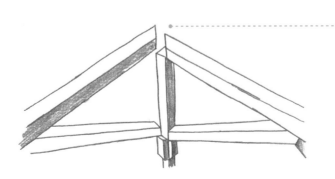

Offer up and fix connecting beam 1 in place with 9½in (240mm) screws. Don't forget to add some glue first.

6

Install connecting beams 2 and 3.
Position connecting beam 2
precisely above the two other posts,
and connecting beam 3 at the far
end between the tips of the two
cross members. Use joist hangers
in both cases; you should use the
internal flange type of joist hanger
for connecting beam 3, as there
will be nowhere on the outside to
screw into.

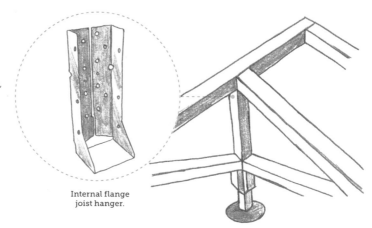

Internal flange
joist hanger.

7

Insert the braces into the cleats
and fasten them securely. The
cleat positions specified in the
plan will make sure the braces
are positioned so that the entire
substructure will automatically
stand true, as long as any
difference in height of the footing
surfaces has been accounted for
previously by cutting the posts to
size (see 3.5). Before installing and

attaching your platform, measure
from each corner to the opposite
corner to obtain the two diagonal
measurements of the substructure.
If these two distances are the same,
the substructure is at right angles
and ready for the platform. If there
is a difference of more than ¼in
(5mm), we recommend correcting
it by simply pushing the elements
of the structure into place.

Job done. All that remains is
to attach the post anchors to their
footings (see 3.4).

Next up is the platform from
page 18 of the plan. Follow the steps
described in section 4.1, beginning
at "What to do on site."

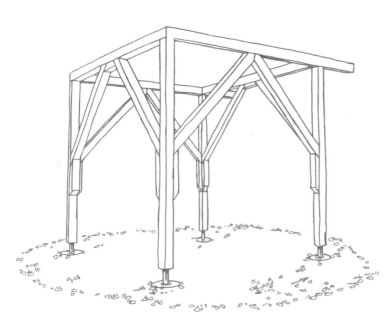

3.8
Substructure with four trees

This section represents a slight digression, or rather an excursion to a location with four trees somewhere on your property. We will show you how such an arrangement might look with a load-bearing beam, and the basic principles demonstrated can be applied to any number of trees. Combine this with the methods we have outlined so far and you will have all the options for a substructure to suit your situation.

1

Let's proceed on the basis that there are some thinner and some thicker trees to choose from. We recommend that you mount the load-bearing beam on the thicker trees (on the left in the illustration) on a fixed bracket, and the one on the thinner trees (on the right in the illustration) on a floating bracket. The thicker ones will move less in the wind than their thinner counterparts, so it makes more sense to mount a floating bracket on the latter so they have room to sway. If your trees are of roughly the same thickness, install the fixed bracket where the heaviest weight is to be supported. The best place for floating brackets is where the least weight is concentrated, because the tree will be less hindered when it sways.

2

This illustration shows one option for accommodating our platform design in such surroundings. The trees will have enough space on all sides even when the treehouse is finally placed on top, and the lengths of the cantilevers are in the safe zone all around.

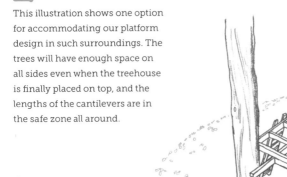

3

As the treehouse itself is fairly tall, the selected platform elevation—just over 8ft 2in (2.5m)—is not especially high, but the top of the roof, at an elevation of 19ft (5.8m), is already getting close to the trunks. It is therefore at a height at which a relatively slim tree with a diameter of 16in (40cm) will begin to move quite violently in strong winds.

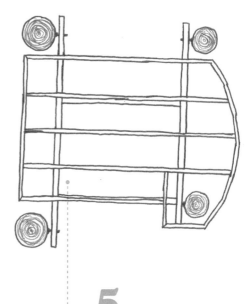

4

Here, too (as shown on page 43), the bolts are located centrally in the trunk, angled toward the axis of the trees and running perpendicular to the load-bearing beam that will lie on top.

5

The load-bearing beam on the right is supported by a fixed bracket and a floating bracket; the load-bearing beam on the left is supported by floating brackets only. This will allow the thinner trees on the right to move more when the wind blows.

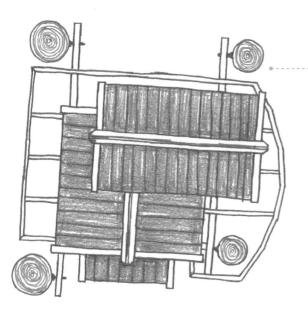

6

Note how sufficient clearance has been left around the trees for growth and movement.

You have a stable base for your platform now that the substructure, the most important foundation for your treehouse, has been laid. Many people feel as if an eternity has passed to get to this point, with not a lot to show for it, but trust us—things will move faster from now on, as you begin building the treehouse itself.

4

Building the Treehouse

4.1
Platform

The next skill to get under your belt is building the platform, then covering it with baseboards so that you can maneuver safely and your treehouse has a flat surface on which to stand. The platform in our build is made from 2×4in (6×12cm) larch joists.

TOOLS

- Basic equipment (see page 22)
- Miter saw
- Workbench
- Chisel
- Batten (minimum 6½ft/2m long) or chalk line
- Plunge saw with guide rail, or circular saw

MATERIALS

- Larch joists, planed and thicknessed to a profile of 2×4in (6×12cm)
- Larch boards 1×8in (2.5×19cm) (for the floor covering)
- Joist hangers: 2¼×4¾in (60×120mm)
- Stainless-steel screws:
  - #10×2¾in (5×70mm)
  - #12×4¾in (6×120mm)
  - #12×5½in (6×140mm)
- Galvanized screws:
  - #12×4¾in (6×120mm)
  - #12×8⅝in (6×220mm)
- Self-tapping screws:
  - #12×9½in (6×240mm)

From now on the kids will be able to enjoy an increasing number of jobs, and in this section they can help with measuring, marking, and doing prep work for you. They can also pitch in by screwing down boards while you lay the floor. They'll have plenty of opportunity to climb the tree and devise their own projects. Make sure children are always safely equipped with a climbing harness and roped when up on the platform.

What to do in the workshop

1

Cut the parts to size as indicated on page 19 of the plan. Make sure you mark each one with its length to avoid any mix-ups later.

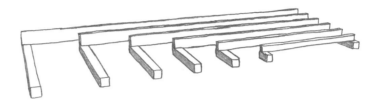

2

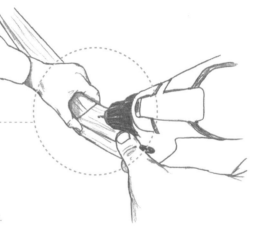

Once the joists are cut to size, use #12×4¾in (6×120mm) stainless-steel screws to fix them together (see plan). Drill a pilot hole with a countersink drill bit so the wood doesn't tear and everything is neat.

3

Smear a little glue on the faces of the miters before screwing them together.

☞ If you are designing your own treehouse, pay attention to the maximum cantilever lengths and/or span widths for the platform. As several adjacent joists will cantilever out parallel to one another (e.g. under the balcony), you can extend the measurements in the illustration on page 35 by about 50 percent. In such cases, the load generated is distributed across several platform joists so that each individual joist supports less weight.

4

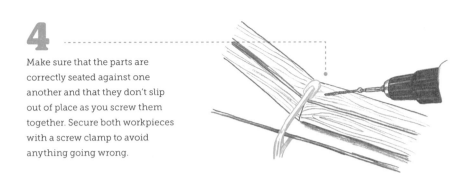

Make sure that the parts are correctly seated against one another and that they don't slip out of place as you screw them together. Secure both workpieces with a screw clamp to avoid anything going wrong.

5

If trees will be growing through the platform, start by screwing together just the parts that make up the the curved edge, leaving the short, straight side open. You will be able to arrange the platform around the tree and close the open part later.

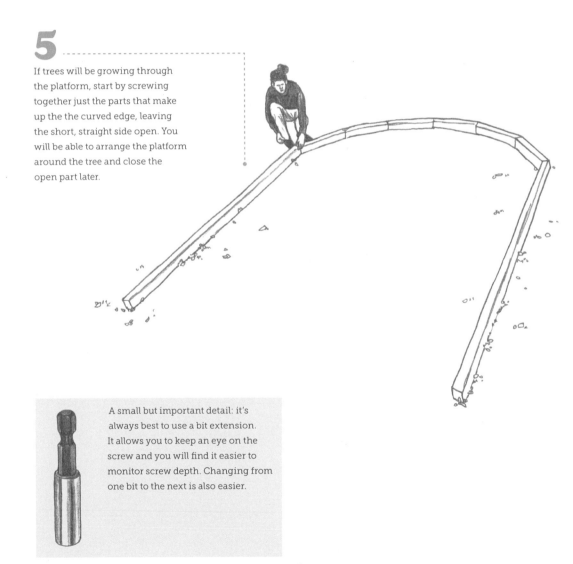

A small but important detail: it's always best to use a bit extension. It allows you to keep an eye on the screw and you will find it easier to monitor screw depth. Changing from one bit to the next is also easier.

What to do on site

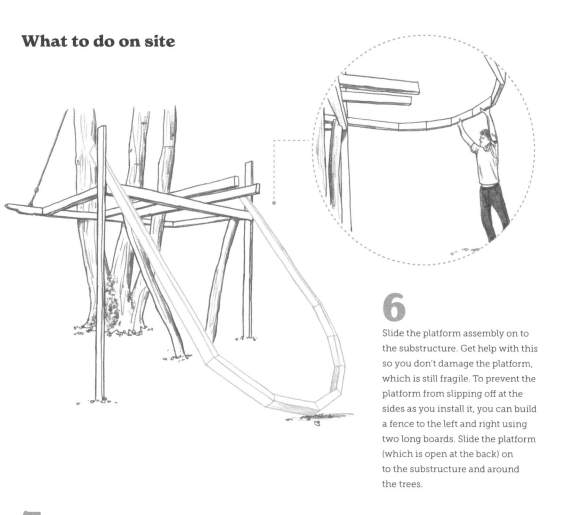

6

Slide the platform assembly on to the substructure. Get help with this so you don't damage the platform, which is still fragile. To prevent the platform from slipping off at the sides as you install it, you can build a fence to the left and right using two long boards. Slide the platform (which is open at the back) on to the substructure and around the trees.

7

Mark the position of the platform on the substructure and slide it into place. The outer straight joists will lie parallel on top of the connecting beams and line up with their outside edges. The platform corners labeled "Corner 1" and "Corner 2" on page 19 of the plan will lie directly on top of the front edge of the cross member of the substructure.

Screw the platform down on the substructure at all points of contact; in our case, this was with #12×8⅝in (6×220mm) screws.

8

Lay the center joints in position (see installation dimensions on page 19 of the plan) and screw them to the front curved edge of the platform. Hold both workpieces in place with a screw clamp; don't forget to glue them first.

9

Drill a pilot hole as before and screw the two workpieces together with 5½in (140mm) stainless-steel screws.

10

Install the remaining parts of the platform as indicated on the plan. If necessary, screw in a board beneath the beam ends as a support and to help you work more easily.

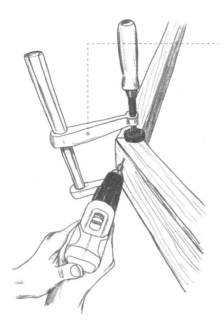

11

Same procedure: glue, clamp tightly, drill a pilot hole, and screw securely.

12

There should be enough clearance around the tree (at least 6in/15cm), to allow it to grow for years to come and sway in the wind.

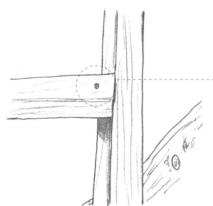

13

At many points in our treehouse, a beam end that has been screwed to another section will also lie on top of the substructure. The connection will be long-lasting and stable as a result.

14

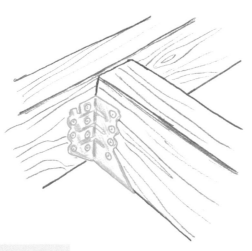

Where this is not the case, reinforce the screw joint with a suitable joist hanger, especially if the weight of a wall is to be applied to that point. Mark the position of the beam and screw in the joist hanger, ideally with self-tapping screws (these have reinforced shanks and heads that are flat on the underside, so they will fit better against the metal of the joist hanger). If you don't want to attach all the screws right away, fix the joist hanger with two screws on each side then lay the beam inside. Fix it to the sides of the joist hanger with two screws on each side. Don't forget to attach the remaining screws once you have all the beams lined up.

☞ You can also attach joist hangers with ring shanks. The advantage (and disadvantage) is that they won't come out again.

15

And you are done! Depending on the substructure you have selected, the platform may look like this. Now return to section 3.4, step 8, and install brace 4, after which you should come back here and continue with the baseboards.

A

B

Or maybe your platform looks like this? If so, you can now continue with the baseboards (see 4.2).

C

Alternatively, your platform could look like this. As above, you can now fit the baseboards.

4.2
Baseboards

Next on the agenda is to lay baseboards on the platform. We chose 1×8in (2.5×19cm) larch boards, but you could use narrower or wider ones.

They should not be any thinner, however, to make sure they do not "cup" or bend when laid over spans of up to 28in (70cm), and will hold their shape better when exposed to wind and weather over long periods.

1

The best place to begin is at the back, at the straight side where the entrance will be. This is a good starting point, especially because the first board will then be a whole one when you install the ladder, and not one that has been ripped to a width of, for example, 1½in (4cm) because that's just how it happened to work out. Line up the first board with the outer edge of the platform and screw it down securely with #10×2¾in (5×70mm) stainless-steel screws. Make sure that it protrudes at one end only; if it's too long, after cutting off the excess you will have a longer piece for which you might find a good use later, but two short pieces will be less useful.

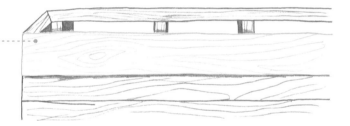

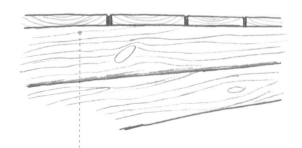

Lay the boards so they are "smiling," i.e. with bark side down and the open side of the growth rings facing up, so they will cup or deform less.

2

Position the screw centrally above the platform joist, leaving about 1¼in (3cm) to the outer edge of the baseboard. If you screw too close to the end, there is a risk that the board will split and need to be replaced. This is especially likely if you don't drill a pilot hole.

Screw the screw into the board until the head is just flush with the top face of the board. The less you screw down the screw, the less water can sit in the screw hole when it rains, averting potential problems. Use the low gear of your cordless drill to control the screw depth more precisely. You can get special depth stops for this, but you should be able to manage these few screws this way without them.

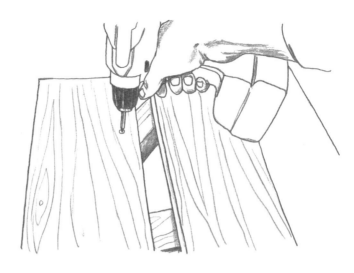

☞ Use a bit extension here too and you will always have a better view of the screw.

3

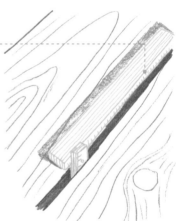

It is best to leave a gap of ⅜in (1cm) between each board you screw down and the next. Use part of a folding ruler, for example, as a spacer, to make sure there are uniform gaps across the whole length of the platform and to allow rainwater to flow away freely without it forming potentially damaging puddles.

4

When laying the boards, if you reach the tree and notice that there is no support for them at that point, cut a joist to size and install it before all the boards are put down. This means they won't be left hanging in the air or susceptible to breaking if weight is applied. Here too, remember to maintain the minimum clearance to the tree of about 6in (15cm).

5

Leave a space around the tree as you lay the boards. To do this, lay out the board to be trimmed and mark out the curvature of the tree.

Cut along the line with a jigsaw and screw the board to the platform.

A 2in (5cm) gap is enough here. Later, you can use the jigsaw to cut around again when the tree has grown a little.

Use a chisel to smooth any torn-out wood fibers along the curve. It will look better and dry more quickly after rain.

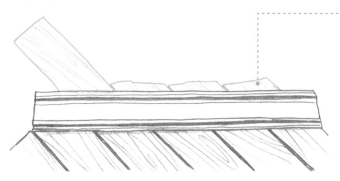

6

Once you have reached the other end of the platform, mark the ends that protrude over the platform edges, using either a straight batten or a chalk line. Cut along the line with a circular saw or make it easier for yourself with a plunge saw and a guide rail; just line it up correctly and cut away.

7

The platform will ultimately look like this. Now grab a camping mat and sleeping bag, and spend a night under the stars on the platform, trying it out and visualizing your treehouse. You might even dream of a few details to incorporate later (this has happened to us a few times).

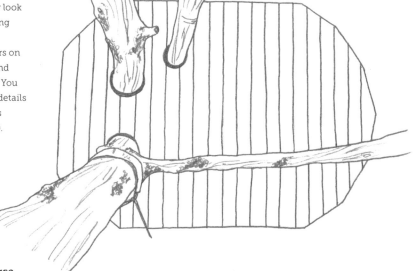

4.3
Walls

Hooray, the platform is up! You may already have spent your first night out under the treetops, done some early morning yoga, or enjoyed an evening drink with friends.

Without a treehouse on top, the platform allows direct contact with the tree and its flora and fauna. Some treehouse-builders, especially if they plan to enjoy their platform in the open air, perhaps as a place for meditation, sports, or music, or as an outdoor bedroom in summer, will stop at this point and skip straight to the sections on handrails and ladders (4.14, 4.15, and 4.16). Others will continue with this section to learn how to assemble the walls of their treehouse.

The walls of our treehouse are all made from spruce studs and posts with the dimensions 2×2in (6×6cm) and 2×4in (6×12cm). Using these has proved to be a stable but relatively light method of building a treehouse. It also allows room for sufficient insulation in the voids between the studs, for example with wood-fiber insulation boards 2in (6cm) thick. The weights of the individual walls are still acceptable, and they will be even lighter if you screw them together only once they are up on the platform, and install the cladding afterward. This also makes it easier to correct any mistakes made when prefabricating the walls. However, applying board cladding to vertical walls at height on a platform is not the easiest task, especially if the wall is right on the edge and requires you to stand on a ladder to work. Make things easier for yourself and assemble the finished walls on the ground. You can make sure that everything fits together and nothing is missing, and you can correct any mistakes that crop up without having to drag everything all the way up to the platform and then down again.

TOOLS

- Basic equipment (see page 22)
- Router with a flush trim bit
- Circular or plunge saw
- Lashing strap (optional)

MATERIALS

- Spruce: solid structural timber with profiles of 2×2in (6×6cm) and 2×4in (6×12cm)
- Batten to use as a ramp when hauling up the walls
- Lower floor purlins from page 41 of the plan
- ¾in (20mm) larch boards for the cladding
- 1in (25mm) larch boards for the exterior window frames
- Stainless-steel screws:
    - #8×2in (4×50mm)
    - #10×2¾in (5×70mm)
- Galvanized screws:
    - #12×4¾in (6×120mm)
    - #12×8⅝in (6×220mm)
    - #12×9½in (6×240mm)
- Compressor
- Nail gun
- Coil stainless-steel nails:
    - 2½in (65mm) (US size 8d)

Erecting the walls and screwing them together will generally take an entire day, but by the end of the day the whole treehouse will suddenly be visible. You will never be as busy again on site as on wall day: all you can see in the morning is an empty platform, but by evening you could be sitting inside with your team, raising a glass to all the work and workers. There's plenty to do before then, though, so get to work!

 Little ones can help you with measuring and marking in the workshop. Children can also practice using a handsaw on the many wall studs, which can be lots of fun if the tool has been correctly sharpened (always with adult supervision, of course!). While you put up the walls, children can help at ground level by monitoring the correct order and helping carry the walls to the ramp. Once all the walls are up, they can help you fit the windows and doors.

A

Here's how the wall framing of the house will look once installed. The wall numbers correspond with those on page 20 of the plan.

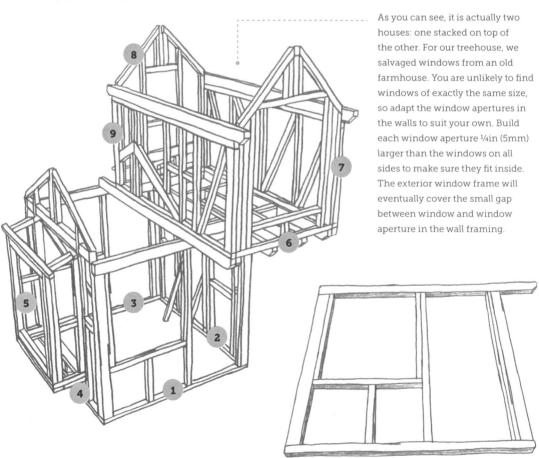

As you can see, it is actually two houses: one stacked on top of the other. For our treehouse, we salvaged windows from an old farmhouse. You are unlikely to find windows of exactly the same size, so adapt the window apertures in the walls to suit your own. Build each window aperture ¼in (5mm) larger than the windows on all sides to make sure they fit inside. The exterior window frame will eventually cover the small gap between window and window aperture in the wall framing.

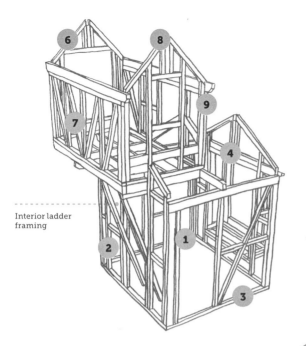

☞ You can build just half the house and do without the upper floor. This will involve half as much work but, of course, deliver half as much space. In this case, replace wall 2 with wall 4. Make two of these; the one on the opposite side will have cladding.

Interior ladder framing

B

This is how it will look if you simply copy the oriel (bay) window for the other side.

C

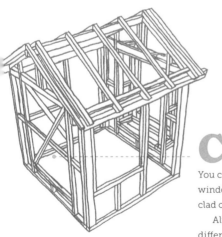

You can also leave out the oriel window on one side and simply clad over the aperture.

Alternatively, build in a different type of window. We would recommend that you make a few small changes to the wall, however, so that the large oriel window aperture is not simply left empty. You could, for example, insert a cross brace into the empty aperture to provide additional stability for the wall. You should then extend the ridge purlin to the right length, cut a few more rafters to size, and adapt the gaps between the rafters so that they are evenly distributed across the width of the roof.

4.4
Wall frames

The structure of the wall frames will generally always be the same: at the base of each wall there is a horizontal sill plate upon which vertical studs are mounted, with cross braces in larger voids to stabilize the structure and make sure everything is at right angles. Inner and outer cladding can be attached to additional braces.

A

A horizontal top plate is installed on the exterior walls, and the eaves purlin is attached to this.

B

The top plates for the gable walls are installed at the angle of the roof. Rafters will be installed on top later.

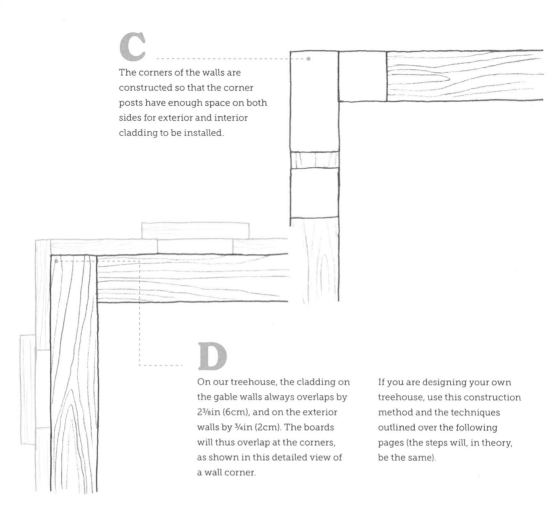

C

The corners of the walls are constructed so that the corner posts have enough space on both sides for exterior and interior cladding to be installed.

D

On our treehouse, the cladding on the gable walls always overlaps by 2⅜in (6cm), and on the exterior walls by ¾in (2cm). The boards will thus overlap at the corners, as shown in this detailed view of a wall corner.

If you are designing your own treehouse, use this construction method and the techniques outlined over the following pages (the steps will, in theory, be the same).

What to do in the workshop

Over the next few pages, we explain how to construct and clad the walls. For now, here's a handy summary of the steps. Read on for fully detailed descriptions of each stage.

1. Cut all the posts and studs for the wall frame to the correct length; don't forget to mark each one for easy identification.

2. Assemble all the wall frames.

3. Screw all the wall frames together to check the fit.

4. Clad all the wall frames.

5. Screw all the clad walls together once again to check for fit.

6. Get it all up on the platform.

Note that there is an exception to this procedure: wall 9 on page 34 of the plan. Fit flashing before installing the cladding; this will serve as a run-off for the lower roof, which meets the wall at this point (see 4.10). Make sure that wall 9 is clad *in situ*, but only after the wall frame has been fixed in place, the flashing is on the roof boards and the membrane of the adjacent roof is in place. You can, however, do a "dry" fit of the cladding boards and cut them to size, which means that all you have to do on the platform is screw them into place. Be sure to number them, since almost all the boards are different lengths and each has a special place.

1

Cut the posts and studs to size for each wall. Lay them out on a large, flat work area and screw them together as illustrated in the plan. Mark each wall with its number from the plan to avoid later mix-ups. You should also mark the outer side to be clad later (in the plan, this is always the side facing you). Set the walls aside. Once all the wall frames have been built, screw the entire house together on the ground—then you'll be able to see if everything fits together before you fit the cladding (it is more difficult to correct any mistakes afterward).

2

When assembling the walls, always precisely mark the positions of the studs relative to one another, referring to the plan. If necessary, use a clamp to hold the two workpieces to be screwed together.

Now you can start putting in the screws. Galvanized 4¾in (120mm) screws are generally the best choice, unless you have to screw into a 4¾in (120mm) post, in which case you will have to use longer screws. You don't generally have to drill pilot holes for these 120mm screws; spruce is relatively soft and doesn't split so easily at these dimensions (2×2in/6×6cm). It's best to drill a pilot hole when using screws longer than 5½in (140mm), however, to ease the strain on your cordless screwdriver.

3

If you are screwing through a 2×4in (6×12cm) stud into another stud that meets it at right angles, the screws should be at least twice as long as the width of 2×4in (6×12cm), i.e. 9½in (24cm). If you don't have any 9½in (240mm) screws handy, drill a pilot hole a few inches/centimeters deep with a drill bit of about the same diameter as the screw head. This is known as a pocket hole. It will reduce the length of the screw in the first stud and allow the threaded portion of the screw to penetrate deeper into the second stud, thereby creating a stable joint.

To fix the screw you will need a bit extension long enough to tighten the screw through the pocket hole and screw it home securely.

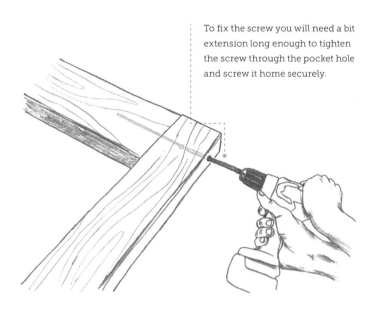

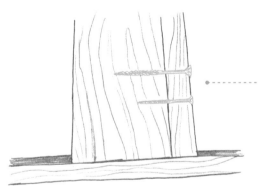

4

With each screw joint, the entire threaded section will ideally end up in the second stud, thereby pulling the first securely into place. See the upper screw in the illustration.

Sometimes, however, this will not be possible (see lower screw), as the screw would simply be too long.

☞ When screwing the walls together, make sure that any markings from the sawmill or supplier are not visible from the inside. If, like us, you do not intend to fit any interior wall cladding, you would need to laboriously sand them off. Leave them facing out where possible, since they will be covered by the exterior cladding.

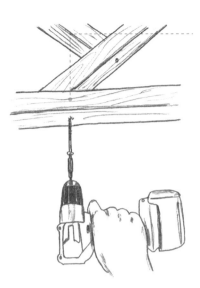

5

If you are screwing into an angled stud, insert the screw as close to perpendicular as possible to the face of the wood. The screw will bite better, and the two workpieces will not shift out of place.

This will sometimes be impossible, in which case, fix both workpieces in place with a clamp once again and screw the screw home. This will prevent the two pieces from shifting.

6

Always drill a pilot hole when making such angled joints; the screw will go in better, and the head of the screw will disappear tidily into the wood without leaving an ugly, ragged hole.

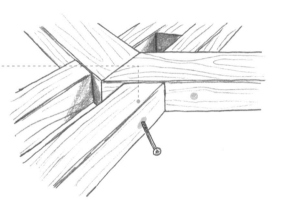

7

Screw a few wall frames together as you go along to check that everything has been cut to the right size and assembled correctly. It makes sense to clad the oriel window wall along with its built-in window, but make sure you can still reach the screws that hold the wall frame together or you will have to heave the whole assembly on to the platform as a unit, and it might be too heavy.

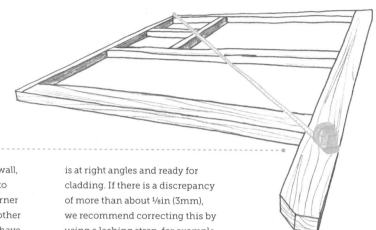

8

Once you have finished a wall, measure from one corner to the diagonally opposite corner and do the same with the other two corners. You will now have two measurements for the two diagonals of the wall. If these two distances are the same, the wall is at right angles and ready for cladding. If there is a discrepancy of more than about ⅛in (3mm), we recommend correcting this by using a lashing strap, for example. The walls will then fit together correctly, and the house will stand true.

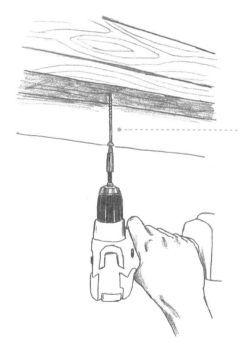

9

Screw the wall to your work surface from underneath. It will now stay in its corrected shape and you can remove the lashing strap and start attaching the cladding.

4.5
Cladding

Here we describe how to clad your house with board and batten cladding. This is made up of two layers: baseboards that are screwed directly to the wall frame as a first layer, followed by a second layer of top boards (or battens). The battens cover the gaps between the baseboards, which are laid at intervals, as shown in the illustration.

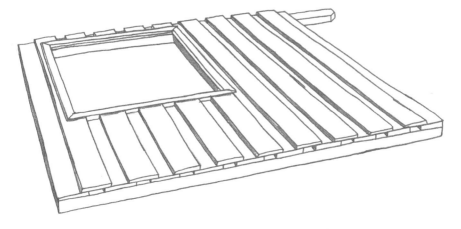

☞ If you want to insulate your house, the wall construction will look slightly different. We recommend installing the cladding on a series of battens to ensure good airflow behind it. To do so, attach a membrane (ideally, a breathable one) to the insulated wall frame, then add the battens followed by the cladding on top.

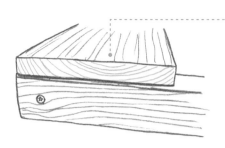

1

The larch boards are again laid "smiling" (i.e. bark side down) to make sure no gaps form between the baseboards and the battens as a result of cupping (see page 90). Begin at one side of the wall, either with an overlap or flush with the edge.

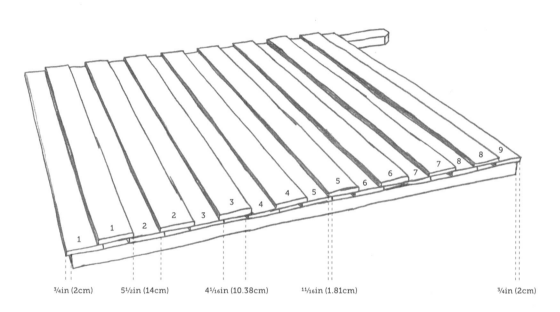

¾in (2cm) 5½in (14cm) 4¹¹⁄₁₆in (10.38cm) ¹¹⁄₁₆in (1.81cm) ¾in (2cm)

2

Calculate the spacing for the baseboards across the entire width of the wall; the gaps will later be covered by the battens. This will involve some measuring and math (we give *our* measurements here, which were in centimeters, but the formula will work in inches as well). First, measure the width of the boards. Ours were 14cm. Each batten on top should ultimately overlap the gap by about ¾in (2cm) on each side, which will give a good fix on the baseboard. You will thus need a gap between the baseboards of about 10cm (14 − [2 × 2]).

To find the exact figure for that gap, determine the width of the wall. Ours was 205cm. Where required, add the cladding overlap at each side; ours was 2cm. The total width to cover with cladding is therefore 209cm.

Divide the total width **TW** (209cm) by the board width **BW** plus the desired gap width **GW1** (14 + 10). The result is the approximate number of baseboards **NB** you will have to lay (8.7). Round it up to a whole number (9 boards) and multiply it by the board width **BW** (14cm). Subtract the result—the

total width of the baseboards **TB**— (126cm) from the total width **TW** (209cm) to find the total width of the gaps **TG**, in our case 83cm.

If you lay 9 boards, you will have 8 gaps, so divide this figure (83cm) by the number of gaps **NG** (in our case, 8). The final result, **GW2** (10.38cm), is the real width of the gap between each pair of baseboards. You will now know how much space to leave between boards to achieve equal spacing across the wall. This will leave you an overlap of 1.81cm, enough to be able to join the boards securely.

In summary, the formula
looks like this:

TW ÷ (BW + GW1) = NB≈
NB × BW = TB
TW − TB = TG
TG ÷ 8 = GW2

Congratulations on getting that
under your belt! You will know
this formula like the back of your
hand by the last wall (if not before),
and find yourself figuring out gap
spacing at every opportunity.

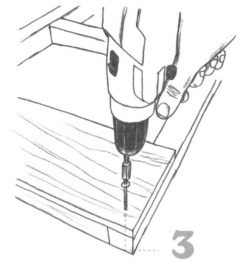

3

Screw each baseboard to the wall
until you reach the other end,
always maintaining the appropriate
spacing; either #10×2⅜in
(5×60mm) or #10×2¾in (5×70mm)
stainless-steel screws are a good
option, or you can use a nail gun
to attach them (this will be a lot
quicker, of course, but you should
use stainless-steel nails for the top
battens, at least).

Seat the screws in the
baseboards close enough to the
edge for them to be covered by
the top board/batten that will later
sit on top. To keep the wood from
splitting, especially at each end, drill
a pilot hole with a countersink bit.

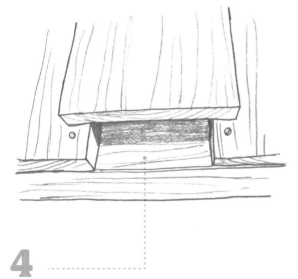

4

Center the battens over the gaps
and fasten them in place.

5

As you clad the walls, you will eventually come up against a window or door aperture. Simply lay the baseboards across these, then cut them out with a circular/plunge saw or trim them with a router. If using the latter, you will need an appropriate router bit, known as a "flush trim" bit, to trim the board flush with the window aperture. You can also cut the boards to a suitable length before fitting them.

Simply follow the inside of the window aperture with the flush trim router. The router will then cut the boards flush with the edge.

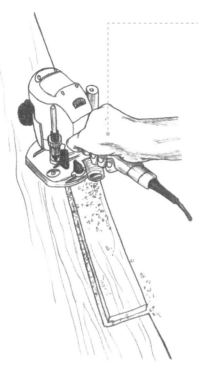

6

If you don't have this practical small tool handy, you can also cut the boards to size with a jigsaw or circular saw, or use a plunge saw with a guide rail. To do this, measure the length of the overlap from the board to the inside edge of the window aperture and mark this on the top side of the board, once on both left and right (and/or once at the top and bottom), so you can use a batten and a pencil to draw a line that you can cut along.

☞ You can of course space the cladding boards irregularly, for a less even look. If you do so, make sure there is sufficient overlap (at least ¾in/2cm) of each batten on each board so the wall stays waterproof. The other key thing to remember is the need to stick to the cladding overlap specified in the plan so that everything ultimately fits together.

7

Use a jigsaw to trim off the short lengths at the top and bottom of the window aperture, cutting up to the marks for the lengthwise rip. Lay the guide rail flush, if you have a plunge saw. Saw carefully from mark to mark.

Trim off the remaining section with the jigsaw.

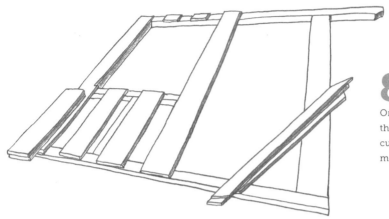

8

Once the baseboards around the window aperture have been cut, fit the window frame before mounting the battens on top.

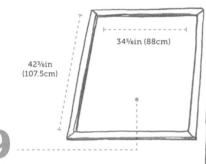

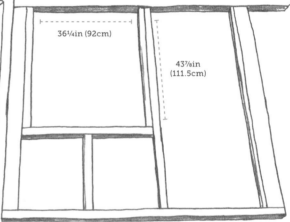

34⅝in (88cm)

42⅜in (107.5cm)

36¼in (92cm)

43⅞in (111.5cm)

9

To determine the internal dimensions of the window frame, deduct 1½in (4cm) in each direction from the dimensions of the window aperture. Use these measurements as the internal width and height of the window frame. The frames will always have ¾in (2cm) clearance on all sides of the window apertures.

10

Build the window frames from slightly thicker material than the top boards/battens (1in/25mm larch boards, for example). The frame should butt up against and stand slightly proud of the battens all around. Cut a miter (a 45-degree angle in this case) for the window frame.

11

Spread a little glue on the mitered faces of the frame sections. Drill a pilot hole using a screw starter with a countersink. Screw the mitered corners together.

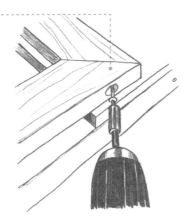

12

Screw the frame to the baseboards with a ¾in (2cm) clearance to the window apertures on all sides. If, like us, you are using windows including frames, the window frame can be used as a stop for the windows, and in addition you will have covered the gap between windows and window aperture. If you are building your own windows, cladding boards will be fitted into the window aperture in section 4.8, and these will butt up perfectly with the window frame.

13

Offer up the top boards/battens and screw them on. Use a circular saw or plunge saw to trim the ends that jut out at the top and bottom of the wall.

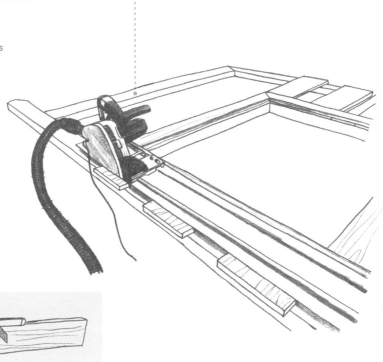

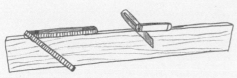

When marking or measuring an angle you have already marked or cut, the best tool to use is a sliding bevel. Alternatively, opt for a folding ruler, but go for the best-quality one for several reasons, especially because it won't slip so easily once it has been set at an angle.

14

Follow the same procedure for the door aperture as for the window aperture, noting that no frame is to be fitted at the bottom, i.e. the threshold: the two framing boards at the side simply run down to the floor. You can leave the door threshold in place (as shown in the illustration) when transporting the wall; then the thinner part of the wall will not wobble. After you have erected the walls, simply saw off the threshold so no one will trip over it later. If you are going to insulate your treehouse, however, leave the threshold in place; the floor of the house will also be insulated and its level will rise by about 3⅜in (8.5cm). You will then need to add a small piece of wood on top of the threshold to make an entrance step for the treehouse.

Building the door is described in section 4.7.

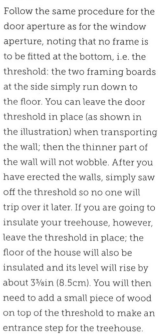

15

Use this method for all the walls, always paying close attention to the measurements on the relevant pages of the plan. Walls with no door or window apertures can simply be boarded out from side to side. Once you have finished all the walls, assemble the house on the ground once again to make sure that all the pieces fit together as they should. It's much easier to fix potential errors on the ground than up on the platform. All done? Fantastic!

☞ There are of course other options for the cladding, such as simple, horizontally overlapping boards, bark boards (where the tree bark is retained at the edge of the board), shiplap weatherboards, and interlocking (tongue-and-groove) boards.

These may be installed slightly differently from the way we outline here, so do some research to find out how to fit the option you choose.

Before screwing together the gable walls (2, 4, 6, and 8) and the side walls with the oriel windows (5, left and right), cut out sections from the top corners of the cladding to accept the purlins. Here are the measurements:

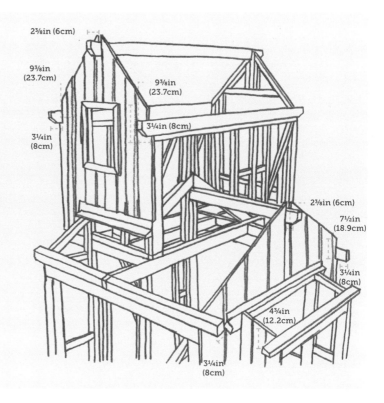

2⅜in (6cm)

9⅜in (23.7cm)

9⅜in (23.7cm)

3¼in (8cm)

3¼in (8cm)

2⅜in (6cm)

7½in (18.9cm)

3¼in (8cm)

4¾in (12.2cm)

3¼in (8cm)

What to do on site

16

Are you sure that all the walls have been correctly assembled and fit together as they should? If so, there's nothing stopping you from erecting the walls on the platform. Take some battens and build yourself a small ramp so you can slide the walls up on to the platform. Make sure to screw the top end of the ramp to the platform to keep it from slipping off as you haul things up.

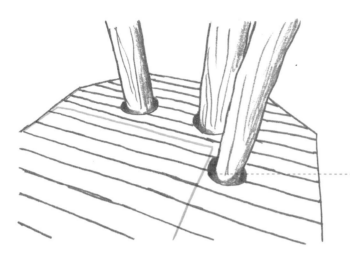

17

Mark the positions of the walls in pencil on the platform before hauling up the walls. Dimensions are on pages 37–8 of the plan.

18

Enlist the help of your team to haul up and install each wall. Figure out the order of the walls in advance to keep them from getting in the way when you assemble them on the platform. Look out for each other. Those at the bottom should let go only when those up top have a secure hold on the wall.

19

Once the walls are on the platform, screw them together with 4¾in (120mm) galvanized screws before even thinking about fastening them to the base. This will allow you to shift them slightly if you need to after measuring the diagonals (see step 22). You should then sink a screw every 24in (60cm) between the walls and between each wall and the base to keep everything together. The piece being attached here is the framing for the interior ladder (see page 114).

20

When hauling up the heavy sections, secure them with a rope or pulley block. Make sure you have a secure footing at every stage, and always keep an eye out for safe exit routes in case sections fall down.

21

The oriel window is in position and is screwed to wall 4 (see box on page 109).

☞ The oriel window—a protruding bay window—is a nice way to extend both your carpentry skills and the feeling of space inside your treehouse. But if you don't want to include it, you can clad the wall fully or build in a standard window. See page 95 for your options.

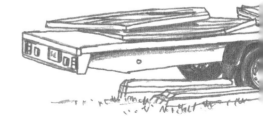

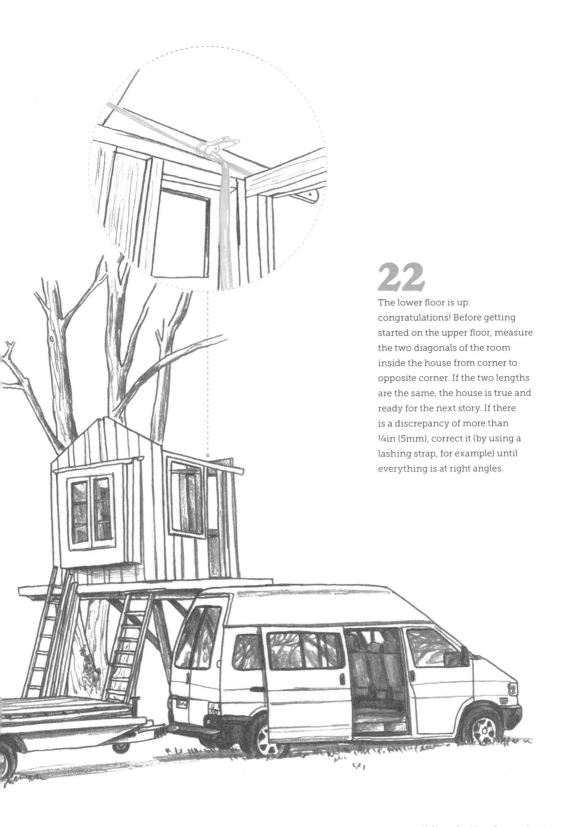

22

The lower floor is up: congratulations! Before getting started on the upper floor, measure the two diagonals of the room inside the house from corner to opposite corner. If the two lengths are the same, the house is true and ready for the next story. If there is a discrepancy of more than ¼in (5mm), correct it (by using a lashing strap, for example) until everything is at right angles.

4.6
Upper floor

If you're happy that your treehouse is true, now is the time to take it upward.

1

Cut the 2×4in (6×12cm) joists for the upper floor to size, as specified on page 39 of the plan. Mark the length of each one for identification purposes on a face that will not be visible later. They all have set positions in the plan and must be screwed to the right place on the lower walls. Make sure you select a screw length double the thickness of the beam.

2

Now it's time to install the ladder to the upper floor. Cut the rungs for the ladder (see page 40 of the plan), and drill centered pilot holes 1¼in (3cm) in from both ends of each one. Screw the rungs in at intervals of 8½in (21.8cm) along the angled beam for the wall ladder, using #12×4in (6×100mm) screws. Use a small level (spirit level) to check that the rungs are all horizontal.

3

Once the joists for the upper floor and the ladder have been completely installed and screwed into position, continue building the upper story. The positions of the upper-floor walls are indicated on page 38 of the plan. Once the walls are up and the roof is waterproof, you can lay the floor at your leisure and whatever the weather; it will be relatively simple and quick to fit (see 5.1).

Upper story

4

It will take a team to lift each wall and install it in its designated position. Make sure you and your assistants always have a secure footing and watch out for each other as you lift and position the walls. Don't make any sudden moves, and do make sure that everyone is aware of where other team members are at all times.

5

As mentioned, wall 9 should be installed with no cladding. Screw it firmly into position, then fit the ridge purlin and eaves purlins for the lower story. To achieve this, insert the ridge purlin into the designated hole in wall 9 and screw 4¾in (120mm) screws down and diagonally into the wall to secure it. All the purlins of the treehouse oversail by 6in (15cm) at the front, measured from the outer edge of the wall frame.

☞ You could also design your own treehouse so that the floorboards are first laid on the upper-floor joists and the upper-story walls then stand on top of these boards—this will give you a larger area to stand and work on when the upper-story walls are installed. We did it differently with our treehouse, working on the principle of "outside skin first, then decorate indoors," but it's a matter of individual choice.

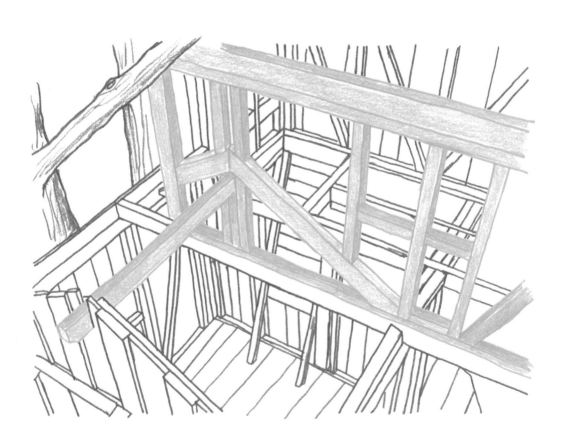

6

During our build, we suddenly found that one side of the upper story was pretty close to the tree. We didn't want to cut off the branch in question, however, since it looked so good growing up over the treehouse. If you encounter the same problem at some point, you may need to correct your work or bend that part of the tree back a little, if you can—or do both. Saw off the branch only when you have considered all other options.

You can use a rope to bend back an intrusive branch and keep it in position by fastening the other end to the trunk. This is better than letting it constantly rub up against the treehouse, damaging its bark and injuring the tree.

If bending back the branch is not effective, attach a thick, solid piece of foam rubber, such as a section of washing machine mat, between the treehouse and the tree at the point where the

branch would otherwise rub. Use several screws to attach the piece of rubber and fix it securely so that it won't slide out of position. You may have to replace it after a while, so install it with this in mind and make it easy to do from the outset. You may have to adjust the roof truss and roof structure a little to accommodate the branch, but we cover that in the appropriate sections.

7

Fit boards to the oriel window seat to make a comfortable spot from which to enjoy the view. Once this is completed, all the walls of the treehouse are up and ready for their roof structure.

4.7
Door

The door welcomes you into your treehouse and can add charm and character. An attractive entrance will spark joy every time you look at it.

Depending on your budget and the nature of your project, build the door yourself, source a second-hand one, or purchase new. We built our door ourselves and used old farmhouse windows that went really well with our friends' home. You can find used doors in local want ads (classifieds), on online auction sites, or at flea markets, garage sales, or salvage yards. Try your local carpenters for new doors.

Kids can assist with cutting and marking in the workshop. They could help cut the posts and boards with a handsaw. Assembling the door and windows, and figuring out a closing mechanism for the door, will be fun for the children; smaller kids will enjoy choosing door latches and hinges.

What to do in the workshop

1

For the door, build a frame out of 2×2in (6×6cm) spruce battens that is ¼in (5mm) smaller all around than the door aperture. In our case, this was 69×173cm (about 175×439in).

2

Make sure you measure the diagonals. It's great if the lengths are the same, but if not, correct the frame until they are identical, then position another 2×2in (6×6cm) batten diagonally and mark the corners.

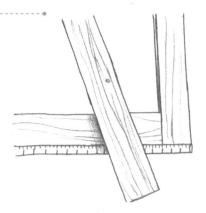

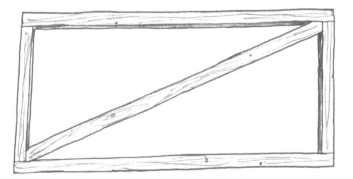

3

Saw along the markings, insert the brace, and screw it to the frame.

4

Now all you need to do is clad the door frame with boards or battens. It's best to do this at the same time as cladding the wall, so you can make sure everything fits together and the door will sit snugly in its frame when closed.

If your treehouse is insulated, the structure of the door will be fundamentally different from the option shown here, in which case, instead of working with a 2×2in (6×6cm) frame, stick two 3-ply panels together and clad the exterior face with larch boards. That way the door will keep its shape over time and form a good seal for as long as possible. This is important, or you will have a gap in the insulation with a constant draft. You should also fit the door with a rebate (a notch that runs around the sides), into which you can stick some weatherstrip (draft excluder) tape; it lasts longer this way, especially on wood. A door made by a carpenter will close most tightly of all, of course, and if you happen to have one of those, adapt the door aperture correspondingly when building the wall frame.

What to do in the workshop or on site

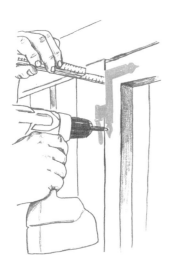

5

Attach the gate hinges or butt hinges you have selected (angled gate hinges with a matching bracket are shown here) to the door and door frame, as shown. Make sure that the specified ¼in (5mm) gap is present between the door and door frame so that the door doesn't rub or stick. Once installed, the diagonal brace in the door should point toward the lower hinge, which will make sure that it does not twist out of shape over time. If you use hinges that prevent the door from being lifted out after installation, fit the door only on site, after the wall has been fitted. Otherwise the wall will be unnecessarily heavy and the door will be a nuisance when you are moving the assembly.

6

If you are fitting the door after the wall has been erected, rest it on spacers ¼in (5mm) thick or on sections of a folding ruler to make sure the door has the clearance required for opening and closing without scraping the floor.

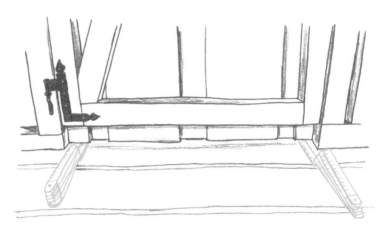

7

You can fit a real mortise lock as a door closer, which means the treehouse can be locked and protected against intruders. A simple version is available that can be screwed to the door, either inside or outside.

Alternatively, a simple cabin hook (A) will work: screw it in, hook it up, job done.

A sliding bolt works too; you can buy standard types from home-improvement (DIY) and hardware stores.

You can also build your own mechanism out of wood (B). Search online (such as YouTube) for easy-to-follow instructions and tutorials for simple (or more complicated) options.

A

B

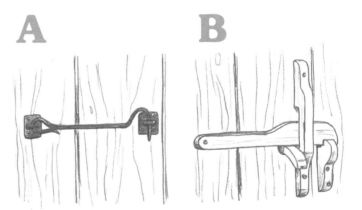

4.8
Windows

The view from the treehouse out on to the world brings a wonderful feeling of being suspended in the heart of nature.

Think about how you would like to frame this view. We recycled old but well-preserved windows from a farmhouse, which were simply beautiful and, arriving complete with frames, also simple to install. With a little luck, you might find some old windows on an online auction site, at a flea market, or perhaps in a dumpster (skip) outside a building undergoing renovation. Such finds are generally affordable (or even free) and will give your treehouse particular charm. Another option would be to install brand new windows made by a carpenter, but these might be very expensive.

Why not just build them yourself? We'll show you a simple version that you can put together relatively quickly with a few battens of wood and panes of (ideally impact-resistant and UV-blocking) Plexiglas. These won't replace a real window in terms of stability and being leakproof, of course, but they will do the job for an uninsulated treehouse. Schedule three to four hours' work per window. You won't need a helping hand, but, as always, please have someone around for safety's sake. When fitting the windows, you will definitely need a second pair of hands, to hold the frames while you screw them in. Instructions for windows of different levels of complexity are available online, on YouTube and elsewhere.

TOOLS
- Basic equipment (see page 22)
- Router
- Table saw
- Glue

MATERIALS
- ¾in (20mm) larch boards
- 1in (25mm) larch boards
- Panes of Plexiglas, impact-resistant and UV-blocking
- Hinges
- Stainless-steel screws:
  - #8×1¼in (4×30mm)
  - #8×2in (4×50mm)
- Casement catches

Kids can be a big help in selecting suitable scrap wood and in measuring and marking. With some assistance, the children can even take over building a whole window. The parts can be cut out with a handsaw.

What to do in the workshop

Rip the boards for the window frames to a width of 2in (5cm), cut them to size, and miter the ends at 45 degrees. The dimensions are the same as for the exterior window frames on the walls, but the windows will be located on the inside of the walls in order to be inward-opening. This simple approach to window building presents two options:

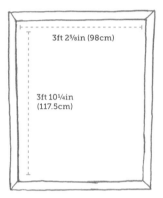

3ft 2⅝in (98cm)

3ft 10¼in (117.5cm)

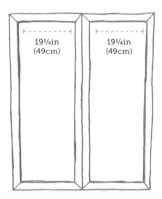

19¼in (49cm)

19¼in (49cm)

 A

Make it in one piece. However, this method would leave the large section a little too unstable for constant opening and closing. In such cases, you are better off screwing it securely to the wall and enjoying it as a fixed window, which is nice to look out of but does not open. Alternatively, make it smaller: it's possible to build an "openable" window up to a width of about 20in (50cm).

B

Make it in two pieces, dividing the window down the middle and creating a double casement. You will have two opening windows— one left, one right—each with two hinges.

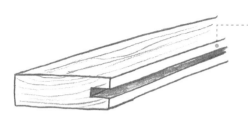

1

For both options A and B, rout a groove ⅜in (1cm) deep in the frame battens for the windowpane. The groove should be exactly as wide as the thickness of the pane, and you can cut it either with a circular saw or with a router and a suitable router bit. If you cut the groove with a circular saw, adjust the blade so that only ⅜in (1cm) protrudes beyond the base. To achieve this you may need to fit a smaller saw blade. Position the fence so that the frame batten is centered over the saw blade. If the blade is thinner than the windowpane, cut the groove in several passes, adjusting the fence a little each time until you get the desired width.

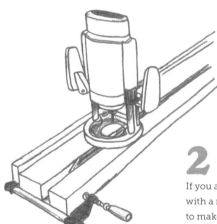

2

If you are going to cut the groove with a router, the best approach is to make a jig out of two battens 2in (5cm) high. You can then slide the router along these.

Use two screw clamps to clamp the frame batten vertically between the jig battens, as illustrated. Screw a board to one side as a fence,

positioning it so that the router bit is precisely centered over the frame batten when the side of the router baseplate is touching the fence (adjust the thickness of the jig batten on that side to achieve this). Now rout a precise groove down the center of the frame batten.

3

Cut the windowpane to a suitable size, i.e. ⅜in (1cm) larger all around than the inside dimensions of the frame. (The illustration shows the double-casement version.)

4

Insert the glass into the groove, smear a little glue on the mitered faces, and screw the frame together using #8×2in (4×50mm) screws.

5

Drill a 45-degree pilot hole into the mitered corners, then carefully screw the frame together.

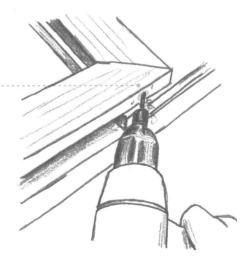

6

If you are making a double casement, screw a stile tongue to one of the two casements. This will cover the gap between the two casements and will give a better seal. Use a board 1½in (4cm) wide, leaving half to overlap.

7

Fit the window apertures with larch boards so that the spruce joists of the wall frame are protected from the weather and to prevent rain from running behind the cladding (it will also look more attractive when complete). Use boards ¾in (2cm) thick and rip them to a width of 4in (10cm). This will make sure they are flush with the window frame on the outside and with the wall studs on the inside.

☞ If, like us, you are using windows with a frame, simply screw through the frame into the window aperture. Drill a pilot hole and use suitable screws to fix them in place.

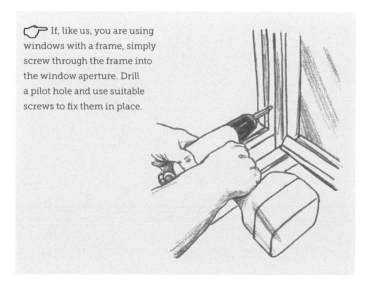

What to do on site

8

Install the double casement windows with a 1¼in (3cm) overlap all around the window aperture. Mark the position on the wall frame in advance; one person can then offer up the window and the other can screw in the hinges. Use small screws (#8×1¼in/4×30mm will be fine). Leave a small gap of about ¹⁄₁₆in (2–3mm) between the casements so that the windows open and close with ease. Sand off the marks later. You can lock the windows simply and easily

with casement catches, which you screw into the wall battens above and below the window. Twist the upper casement catches down and they stop the window from opening, and vice versa for the lower casement catches: simple and effective.

The single casement version should also overlap by 1¼in (3cm) on all sides. Screw it to the wall batten, leaving regular intervals of about 20in (50cm) between screws.

4.9
Roof truss

Now that the walls are up, you are no doubt feeling excited that completion is getting closer. Does the treehouse feel more real and tangible?

Next up is building the roof assembly. We felt a gabled (or apex) roof looked more appealing than a pent (single-slope) roof, and it was what Leni wanted, too. It does require a little more effort to build, but the advantage of a gabled roof is that the maximum standing height is in the center, giving you slightly greater leeway when designing the interior decor and allowing you to move around more easily inside (especially in a not particularly tall house). Schedule an entire weekend for this stage of the project.

TOOLS
- Basic equipment (see page 22)
- Tin snips (optional)
- Lashing strap

MATERIALS
- Spruce: solid structural timber with cross sections of 2×2in (6×6cm) and 2×4in (6×12cm)
- Roofing film and flashing to waterproof any cut-out sections where branches may be in the way (optional)
- #12×4¾in (6×120mm) galvanized screws

☞ With a roof as small as that of your treehouse, you can install the rafters without cutting notches (known as "birdsmouths") for roof pitches of up to about 30 degrees. For stability, you should cut birdsmouths for roof pitches greater than 30 degrees. This will mean that the weight of the roof will not rest solely on the screw joint between the rafters and purlins, but will be transmitted vertically down on to the walls. When cutting birdsmouths, do not "overnotch": always make sure that enough wood remains directly above the birdsmouth, i.e. at least half the height of the rafter, so that the birdsmouth is not weakened.

This is how the roof truss will look once you have finished this section. Note the small rafters for the oriel window to the left.

 Kids can help in the workshop with measuring and marking. As with the walls, there will be opportunities for them to cut 2×2in (6×6cm) timber with a handsaw. Installing the roof truss on site comes with potential hazards, so get the child(ren) involved elsewhere. Depending on age and ability, they could take charge of designing a door sign, carving a goblin or troll to guard the treehouse, or getting materials and tools ready.

The roof truss of our treehouse is made up of purlins and rafters. The eaves purlins lie on top of the sides of the house, on the exterior walls, while the ridge purlin is at the top of the gable walls. These purlins work together to hold up the rafters on which the roof boards will be laid.

A membrane will then be laid on top of the roof boards as a second waterproof lining, upon which the tin roof is installed. The roof will ultimately have eaves of about 6–8in (15–20cm) all around to make sure that the rain drips off, rather than running back into the house.

If you are designing your own treehouse, you should also plan to include these eaves and make sure the rafters are not spaced more than 28in (70cm) apart. This will ensure that the roof boards lying on top are weight-bearing and won't bend or break.

What to do in the workshop

1

Cut all the purlins, rafters, and spacers to size as described on pages 41–7 of the plan. Mark them up on faces that will later be hidden and wrap them up into small bundles for ease of carrying.

What to do on site

2

Before proceeding with building the roof truss, you know what you must do: yes, you guessed it, measure the diagonals. If the lengths aren't the same, pull everything true with a lashing strap, as before.

First install the ridge purlin on which the rafters will later be laid. Mark the eaves overhang of 6in (15cm) on the purlin then hammer it into position, using a block of wood to stop the hammer from damaging the end of the beam.

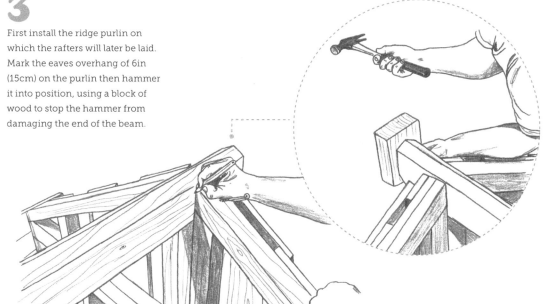

4

Screw the purlin securely to the gable walls before installing the eaves purlins in the same way. Mark the positions of the rafters on the ridge purlin. Make a cross on the side of the marking where the rafters are to be fitted to make sure you screw the rafter into place on the correct side. This will depend on whether you are measuring the clearance (the spaces between the rafters) or the distance from the left-hand side of one rafter to the left-hand side of the next (right side to right side is of course fine too). In the image, the first measurement is the clearance (i.e. 21½in/55cm), while the subsequent measurements of 24in (61cm) are for the spacing.

5

The spacers will dictate the spacing on the eaves purlins by filling the gaps between the rafters. Install the rafters in their marked positions, being sure to alternate: rafter, spacer, rafter, spacer. This will guarantee that the gaps are correct. Always begin with the rafters on one gable wall and work down the full length of the wall to the opposite gable wall.

6

The rafters for the upper story look
as shown at right, and the rafters
for the lower story as shown at
lower right. The rafters for the lower
floor have no birdsmouths, i.e. no
defined point at which they lie on
top of the eaves purlin. However, on
page 43 of the plan you will see that
the distance from the upper end of
the rafter to the inner side of the
wall frame on which the rafters sit
is 46⅜in (117.8cm), measured along
the underside of the rafters. Mark
this length on the long rafters. This
will guarantee that the position of
the rafters on the walls is correct
during assembly, and that the walls
will stand vertically.

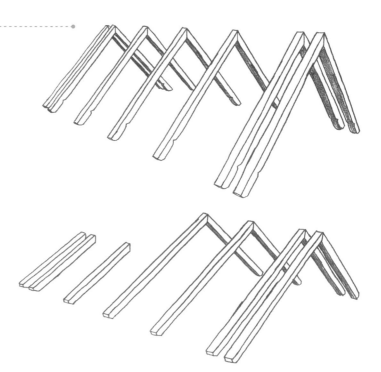

7

Screw the rafters to the purlins
using maximum 4¾in (120mm)
screws, always making sure that
the screws don't poke through
underneath. Once the roof boards
have been laid on top, you won't be
able to take them out again. Here
you see the rafters with spacers
between them.

8

If you got too close to the tree when you were putting up the walls, you may encounter the same problem with the roof.

9

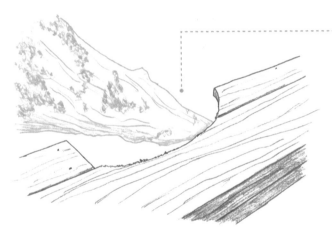

If this is the case, saw off a small section of the roof boards at the appropriate spot so that the trunk or branch has enough space. You can seal the spot up again with roofing film or flashing; you might have to improvise, like we did. We explain how we managed to get the spot sealed up again in the next section (see steps 9–11).

10

Things are simpler at the corners of the roof: here it is often enough to use a handsaw to trim an inch or so (a couple of centimeters) off the corner in question.

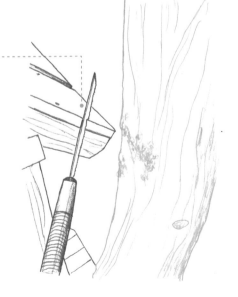

4.10
Roof

What would a treehouse be without a roof? Nothing more than a leaky wooden vessel for the colorful mixed-leaf salad that falls from the trees in the autumn. What it needs is to be sealed.

It's time to put the cherry on your cake: the roof. You will need an assistant in the workshop and two more on site, and you would be wise to schedule a whole weekend for this stage of the project. If, like us, you find even a single branch that is located too close to the treehouse, extra time will be needed to accommodate it. We chose corrugated (box-profile) sheeting to roof our treehouse as it is easy to lay, widely available, and long-lasting—if carefully installed. Also consider whether the color you choose will blend in with the treetop. Other options for covering the roof appear on page 144.

 Kids can help in the workshop with measuring and marking, and, to a certain extent, take charge of cutting the boards for roof and porch areas with a handsaw. Extreme caution is advised when installing the tin roof, and children are safer on the ground during this stage of the proceedings. If you have chosen wooden shingles to cover the roof, children can lend a hand with laying them; stable scaffolding as a secure work platform is a prerequisite.

TOOLS
- Basic equipment (see page 22)
- Nibbler or tin snips
- Hammer tacker

MATERIALS
- ¾in (20mm) timber for the roof boards, e.g. spruce or larch, planed or unplaned
- Larch boards for the porches (1×8in/2×19cm)
- Roof battens, 1×2in (30×50mm) (optional—you can screw the corrugated/box-profile sheeting directly to the membrane with no battens, as we did; see page 140)
- Corrugated (box-profile) sheeting
- 6½ft (2m) flashing
- 1 roll breathable membrane or roofing felt and clout nails
- Staples for the hammer tacker
- Waterproof duct tape
- Galvanized screws:
  - #10×2⅜in (5×60mm)
- Stainless-steel screws:
  - #10×2¾in (5×70mm)
- Roofing (Spengler) screws

What to do in the workshop

1

Cut the lumber (timber) for the
roof boards and porches to size.
You could also cut the membrane/
roofing felt at this stage; it is best to
leave the pieces a little larger than
the roof surface, then trim off the
excess with a utility knife (Stanley
knife) as you lay them. Also cut the
corrugated (box-profile) sheeting to
size. See roof surface dimensions
on page 48 of the plan.

What to do on site

2

Once the wood is cut to size,
screw or nail the roof boards to
the rafters. For our treehouse,
we began by laying a roof board
lengthwise (marked **x** on the
illustration for step 3) between the
outermost rafter (known as the
"fly rafter"; on the far left in the
illustration below) and the next
one in, which lies on top of the
wall. This means we didn't have
to work with little lengths of wood
and the whole thing looked neater.
The board, at 7in (18cm), is just
wide enough to reach the center
of the second rafter when laid
lengthwise, leaving sufficient space
on the rafter to support the rest
of the boards, which will be laid
perpendicular to it.

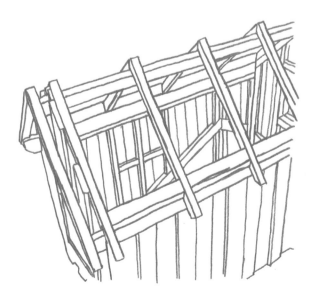

3

Start laying the horizontal boards at the bottom of the roof, flush with the end of the rafters, laying each on top of the last and using two screws to fix it to each rafter beneath. When you reach the ridge rafter, you will probably have to rip the last board to size to fit in the gap.

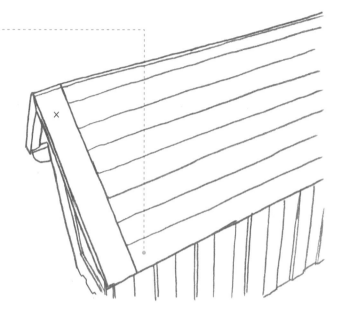

4

Now it's time to to take care of the flashing between wall 9 and the lower roof. First, cover the lower-story roof with boards as described above, beginning at the bottom, flush with the ends of the rafter. Work toward the top, laying each board in turn and fixing it to the rafters using #10×2¾in (5×70mm) screws, or nails of a suitable size.

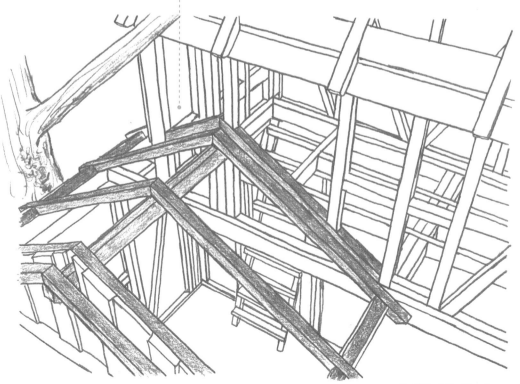

5

Make sure that you always hit the
rafter below or you will end up with
dangerous screw tips or nail points
sticking out of the roof. When
you reach the roof ridge, you will
probably have to rip the last board
to size to fit in the gap.

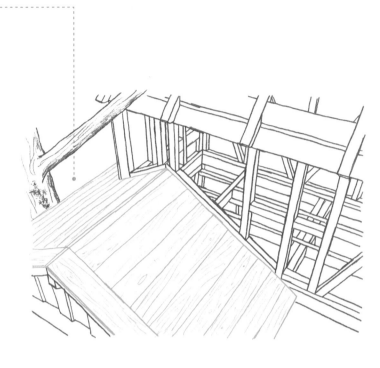

6

Once both sides have been clad,
it's time to fit the membrane or
roofing felt. First, cut it to size
if you haven't done so already,
leaving a little excess on all sides.
Fix the membrane in place with
a hammer tacker, using as few
staples as possible: unnecessary
holes are potential leak points in
the roof. If you are using roofing
felt, go for clout nails, which have

wider heads, and, again, use as
few as possible. The tin roof will
be fitted on top of this later, so at
least it won't blow away. Leave an
overlap of a few inches/centimeters
in the membrane or roofing felt on
wall 9 to create a small, waterproof
channel at the junction of the wall
and the roof. This will allow any
water that manages to penetrate
to run down the membrane.

☞ Roofing (Spengler) screws have a little
integrated washer with a rubber gasket that seals
the hole made by the screw. When fitting the
screw, make sure it is properly seated, but do not
overtighten or you will damage the rubber.

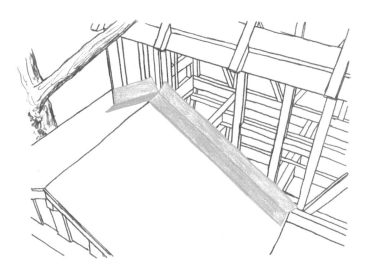

7

Now it's time to fit the flashing. L-shaped lengths of flashing already bent at a 90-degree angle are available from home-improvement (DIY) stores, and you can cut them with tin snips or an electric nibbler. Identify the side that will stand up vertically from the top of the roof and cut through it down to the middle so you can then bend the flashing down on to both sides of the roof. Screw it to the wall timbers with three or four roofing (Spengler) screws. You can fix the lower side in place later in conjunction with the corrugated (box-profile) sheeting.

8

Finish cladding wall 9 and continue to fit the other roof sections.

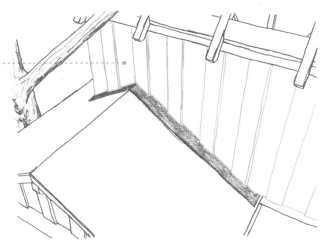

9

We cut out a section of the roof at the spot where a branch was growing too close to the house and sealed the area with flashing and membrane. We had previously tied the branch back lightly with a rope to stop it from touching the house.

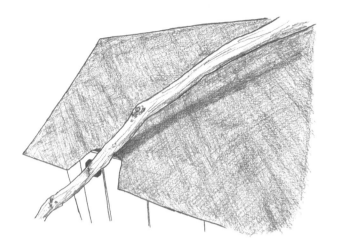

10

Once you have laid roof boards in all the necessary locations, cover the entire roof with the membrane and/or roofing felt. Start with one course along the bottom of each side of the roof and lay a second course over the roof ridge. Given the small size of the roof, you will then have a leakproof roof with a decent overlap between the two layers of membrane/roofing felt. Fix these securely in place with a staple gun, folding the edges over a little, and you are done.

11

Carefully cut a few inches/ centimeters of overlap in the membrane or felt for the cut-out section at the point where the branch is in the way.

Continue by fitting battens and counter-battening, or attaching the tin roof directly, with no battens, as we did.

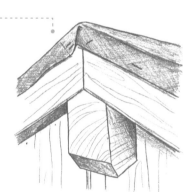

PROS FOR THE VERSION WITH BATTENS. The space under the roof is better ventilated and water cannot form puddles that could shorten the lifespan of the roof.

PROS FOR THE VERSION WITHOUT BATTENS. This is much less complicated and the roof will be leakproof even without battens. You don't necessarily need ventilation under the roof since the house is not insulated, and any waterlogging will dry out quickly. The noise of rain on the tin roof will be quieter with no battens.

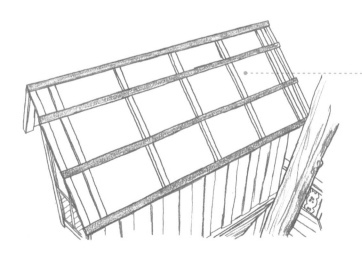

If you intend to fit battens, first screw the counter-battening in place, i.e. one batten along each rafter. You will be screwing the battens on to these at right angles, with a maximum spacing of 16in (40cm). Begin at the bottom and work your way up to the ridge assembly at the top. You will ultimately attach the corrugated (box-profile) sheeting to these battens.

4.11
Corrugated sheeting

1

The corrugated (box-profile) sheeting should oversail the fascia boards beneath by 1¼in (3cm) for rainwater to drip off effectively. To calculate the amount of sheeting required, divide the width of the roof by the width of the sheeting sections, factoring in two ridges of overlap from sheet to sheet. This is required to make sure the roof doesn't leak. Measure, then strike a line with a straight batten. Remember when measuring that the sheeting will be laid with the ridges running vertically from eaves to ridge.

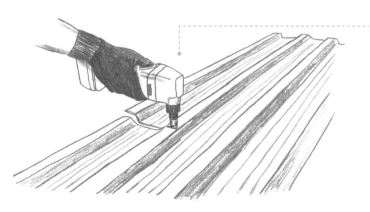

2

Cut the sheeting to size. A cordless nibbler is much more comfortable to use than tin snips, especially for longer cuts. Never use an angle grinder to cut corrugated sheeting because the sparks will burn small holes in the coating, which may rust more quickly.

⚠ The edges of the sheeting are extremely sharp, so wear rubberized work gloves for this part of the project.

3

Essentially, the screws that attach the sheeting to the roof can be fixed through what are known as the "crowns" or the "troughs," i.e. through the middle of the ridges (high) or the valleys (low). For flat roofs or low-profile sheeting, we recommend crowns; for steep roofs or deeper sheeting profiles, it should be troughs. We chose to fix the screws through the crowns largely because our long roofing (Spengler) screws would have come out at the other side of the roof boards if we had done it through the troughs.

When fixing screws through the crowns, be sure to screw in straight; don't overtighten and don't crush anything. This is best achieved by fitting a large gasket (>¾in/19mm) or a suitable hemispherical spacer beneath the sheeting.

When fixing screws through the troughs, also be sure to screw straight and not overtighten.

Sheeting and appropriate fixings are available from home-improvement (DIY) stores. This illustration shows the recommended screw spacing for the sheeting.

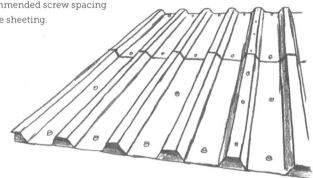

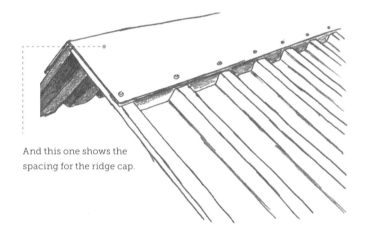

And this one shows the spacing for the ridge cap.

4

The area with the branch ended up looking like this when the corrugated sheeting was fitted. The sheeting was trimmed in such a way that it still oversailed the trimmed roof boards beneath it as much as possible. We then blunted the edge of the sheeting with some rubber (an old bicycle tire or similar will do the trick) that we attached with assembly adhesive. The branch is still quite close to the house, but this should work.

4.12
Bargeboards

1

Mount the bargeboards as shown on pages 49–52 of the plan. These will add extra waterproofing to the roof (even against driving rain) by covering up the ends of the gables. The roof cladding will also be resistant to strong wind.

Use #10×2⅜in (5×60mm) screws to fix the side boards to the fly rafters. The top edge of each board should be flush with the top edge of the roof sheeting.

2

Next, screw the top boards on to the bargeboards from above, leaving a slight overhang on the outside (#8×2in/4×50mm screws will suffice). Put a folding ruler, for example, against the barge board (see illustration) and let the top board overhang the bargeboard by the width of the ruler—this will reproduce the ⅝in (16mm) overhang from the plan simply and with no measuring.

3

Screw the fascia boards to the ends of the rafters, leaving the oversail of the sheeting above so that water can flow away. Since you are screwing into end grain here, use screws that are long enough, i.e. at least #10×2¾in (5×70mm).

4.13
Alternative roof coverings

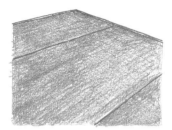

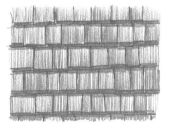

Fiberglass (bitumen) shingles

These are generally available in red, green, and anthracite. They are easy and quick to fit and will work on all roofs up to a pitch of 15 degrees.

+ affordable and durable option

+ simple to fit

– not particularly eco-friendly

– generally not as attractive as other options on treehouses

Roofing felt or built-up roofing

Roofing felt doesn't take long to fit but is more suitable as sheeting (another layer of covering will be laid on top). It is really only suitable as a temporary roof covering. While built-up roofing is more durable and is suitable for flat roofs, it must be heated with a blowtorch and applied by someone with appropriate expertise.

+ affordable option

+ simple to fit

– not very durable

– generally not as attractive as other options on treehouses

Wooden shingles

These are available in a range of types and qualities (larch, oak, and red or white cedar, and sawn or split). This is the most attractive method for roofing a treehouse in our opinion, because it is the best way to tie the structure visually into its natural surroundings. However, fitting shingles is hard work and is recommended only for roof pitches of 22 degrees or more if no other measures are taken to seal the roof.

+ visually appealing

+ very durable

+ eco-friendly (renewable)

– expensive

– complicated to fit

☞ For fiberglass (bitumen) shingles and built-up roofing, refer to the relevant manufacturer's installation instructions to discover how each method works. Fitting wooden shingles to a roof or even a wall is more complicated, and there are several factors to keep in mind if you want to be certain of a leakproof roof over the long term. Your shingle supplier should give you a few pointers, and there are plenty of books and websites that can help too.

4.14
Handrail

We wanted to leave you lots of space for your ideas, so this handrail features gaps between the uprights for you to fill with your own design.

We recycled ornamental boards dismantled from an old farmhouse for ours, with the owner's permission, of course. We then screwed them into place in the space between the posts. Of course, you can also simply use larch balusters (1×2in/25×45mm) or thick and robust branches (ideally oak or another hardwood); cut your own ornamental boards; or create something with rope. Just make sure that everything is solid and secure, and the gaps between the individual elements are no larger than 4in (10cm) to prevent small children from getting their heads stuck.

TOOLS

- Basic equipment (see page 22)
- Miter saw

MATERIALS

- Larch battens, 3×3in (7×7cm)
- Larch boards, 1in (25mm) thick, for the top handrail
- Larch boards, 1×8in (2×19cm), for the inner and outer support boards and the top and bottom rail; or larch battens, 1×2in (25×45mm)
- Stainless-steel screws:
  - #10×2⅜in (5×60mm)
  - #12×4¾in (6×120mm)
  - #12×5½in (6×140mm)

 Kids can help with measuring and marking in the workshop. Using a handsaw reaches the next level of difficulty now; instead of the spruce they have used so far, they will be sawing larger cross sections of larch, which is more likely to get them sweating. Children can also take charge of designs for filling in the gaps between the posts, but make sure that the results are durable and robust.

What to do in the workshop

1
Cut all the materials for the individual parts of the handrail to size as described on pages 53–9 of the plan and mark up each piece on a part that will not be visible later. The inner and outer rail supports and the top and bottom rails can all be ripped from 1×8in (2×19cm) larch boards, or you can use 1×2in (25×45mm) larch battens.

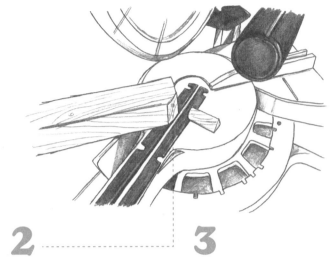

2
Cut a 45-degree miter off the bottom ¾in (2cm) of the lower ends of the posts, which will look better than a 90-degree cut.

3
Assemble the parts of the handrail as detailed in the plan. The inner rail support always protrudes by ¾in (2cm) beyond the posts on either side, but this may vary with the outer support; see the plan for details.

4
Mark the points at which the sections of handrail overlap (refer to the relevant page of the plan).

You should always drill a pilot hole in the narrow boards so they don't split. Make sure you assemble everything at right angles.

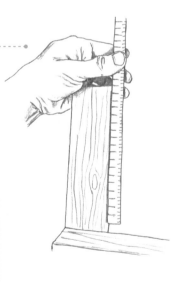

☞ If you cut the top handrail for several sections of railing in sequence from one long board, it will have a continuous grain and, once sanded to a fine finish, will almost appear to have been made from a single piece of wood.

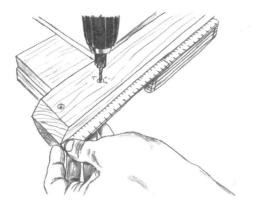

5

Fix the handrail sections to the inner and outer support boards using #8×2in (4×50mm) screws. Maintain regular spacing of 1¼in (3cm) from the screws to the edge to prevent splitting and make the screws look even.

6

Drill pilot holes for the screws to attach the posts to the platform. The platform is 4¾in (12cm) high, so locate the upper screw no higher than 4in (10cm); this makes sure that it will have enough wood to bite into and hold the handrail securely. Locate the lower screw just above the 45-degree cut, i.e. 1¼in (3cm) above the end of the post.

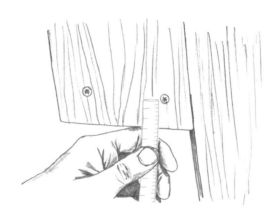

What to do on site

7

The pre-assembled sections of the handrail should now be installed in the appropriate places. Add a little glue between the posts and the platform for extra stability.

One person should hold the pieces steady as the other screws. The posts must be flush at the bottom with the lower edge of the platform, and at the sides there must always be a gap of ¾in (2cm) to the corners of the platform.

Continue installing evenly, section by section.

8

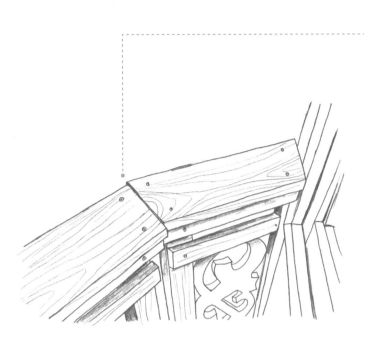

Don't worry if there is a slight
difference in height at the top;
you can sand it flat.

Don't forget to add a dab of glue
between the sections of railing.
Then drill a pilot hole and screw the
sections together with #10×2¾in
(5×70mm) screws.

9

Here's how our finished
handrail looks.

4.15
Other handrail options

For those who have something different in mind from our version with ornamental boards, here are a few alternatives.

Ropes

These can be either strung horizontally or threaded from top to bottom between the posts. Either option can be attractive, especially if you use hemp-colored rope (always use robust polypropylene rope, however, as actual hemp rope won't last long with constant exposure to the weather). You should also remember that rope strung horizontally will be an invitation to small children to climb it like a ladder, so it may represent a hazard.

Branches

These look appealing and organic as a treehouse railing, and will tie the treehouse visually into its surroundings. Install them at regular intervals, spaced a maximum of 4in (10cm) apart, or mix them up randomly so that they look like a big bird's nest. With the bird's-nest option, the maximum interval spacing of 4in (10cm) is still essential, and stick to using branches with a minimum diameter of 1¼in (3cm). Be sure to use branches that are in good condition, ideally hardwood from deciduous trees. These will undoubtedly be more durable without bark, as they will dry out more quickly, but they look a little better with their bark.

Balusters

These can be installed vertically between the posts at maximum intervals of 4in (10cm). They are attractive, simple, and long-lasting.

4.16
Ship's ladder

Your treehouse is almost finished. All you're missing is the link between heaven and earth.

One of the most attractive but relatively easy ways to build a stairway to this particular heaven is the ship's ladder, which has an integrated handrail to grip as you climb. You can do a lot of the prep work on your own, but you will need one helper during installation (at the latest), otherwise things can get very tricky. You should schedule a whole day for this stage of the project.

 Kids can help with measuring and marking in the workshop and can also take charge, to some degree, of cutting the parts. They should be pros in the use of a handsaw by now. They can also be involved with assembling the ladder at the end of the day. Once it is installed, even very little ones (with your help and under supervision, of course) can scramble up and down the ladder to inaugurate it.

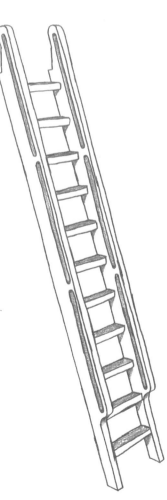

TOOLS
- Basic equipment (see page 22)
- Jigsaw
- Circular saw/plunge saw or circular table saw
- Router with roundover bit
- ½in (12mm) drill bit
- 1¼in (30mm) Forstner bit
- Angle grinder
- Pair of compasses, or two round objects, one with a diameter of 1¼in (3cm) and one with a diameter of 3½in (9cm)
- Spade
- Shovel
- Pickaxe
- Trowel
- Robust mortar tub or large bucket for mixing
- Fast-setting or standard concrete
- Mixing attachment for power drill

MATERIALS
- Larch battens, 2×8in (5×20cm)
- ⁷⁄₁₆in (12mm) wooden dowels
- L-shaped post anchors
- #12×4¾in (6×120mm stainless-steel screws
- M12 threaded rods with suitable washers and nuts
- #12×2in (6×50mm) waferhead screws

What to do in the workshop

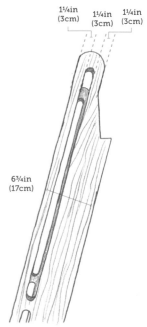

1¼in (3cm) 1¼in (3cm) 1¼in (3cm)

6¾in (17cm)

1
Cut all the parts to size as described on page 60 of the plan. Rip them to the prescribed width as required and lay them out in your work area.

2
First up is the handrail of the ladder and/or the top railing. This will be 1¼in (3cm) wide, as will the slot beneath it. Each side rail will be 6¾in (17cm) wide in total, leaving a space of 4¼in (11cm) to install the rungs between the side rails.

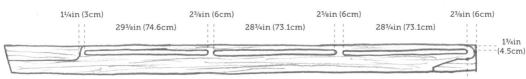

1¼in (3cm)   2⅜in (6cm)   2⅜in (6cm)   2⅜in (6cm)

29⅜in (74.6cm)   28¾in (73.1cm)   28¾in (73.1cm)

1¾in (4.5cm)

3
Lay the first side rail out in front of you on the workbench. Mark out the locations for the drill points as indicated above.

PROCEDURE
- Measure 2⅜in (6cm) in from the right-hand end of the side rail then measure down 1¾in (4.5cm) from the top. Mark this point.

- From this point, measure 28¾in (73.1cm) to the left and again 1¾in (4.5cm) down from the top. Mark.

- From this point, measure 2⅜in (6cm) to the left and again 1¾in (4.5cm) down from the top. Mark.

- From this point, measure another 28¾in (73.1cm) to the left and again 1¾in (4.5cm) down from the top. Mark.

- From this point, measure another 2⅜in (6cm) to the left and again 1¾in (4.5cm) down from the top. Mark.

- From this point, measure a final 29⅜in (74.6cm) to the left and again 1¾in (4.5cm) down from the top. Mark.

4
Using a pair of compasses, draw a circle of 1¾in (4.5cm) radius, centered on the first marked point at the right-hand end of the side rail. Saw along the line with a jigsaw; this will give you a beautifully rounded railing end. If you don't have compasses, use any object with a diameter of 3½in (9cm).

5

Drill a hole at each of the marked points with a 1¼in (30mm) Forstner bit, then join up the outer edges of the holes with a line along which to cut out the slots. If you have a plunge saw with a guide rail, line this up directly with the outer edges of the holes and make a cut. Remember to include the thickness of the saw blade so you get a flowing transition between the round hole and the straight cut. Leave the small sections between the holes intact and don't cut through them by mistake; clearly mark each point at which you must stop cutting. You won't be able to cut right up to the hole with the plunge saw, so saw the last little bit with a jigsaw or handsaw.

☞ To avoid tearing or splitting the wood of the side rail when the drill bit goes through, place a scrap board beneath the point where you are drilling.

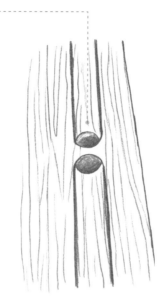

6

Use a router with a roundover bit to "knock the corners off," i.e. rout them down until they are rounded off to make the handrail smooth to the touch. To do this, simply slide the router along the slots in an evenly paced pass.

To make the handrail even smoother to handle, sand the side rails with an orbital sander and a 120 grit disc; this will also remove any burn marks from sawing or routing.

7

Repeat all these steps for the second side rail. You can also simply make the second rail as a copy by laying the first on top of the wood and tracing the outline, as shown here.

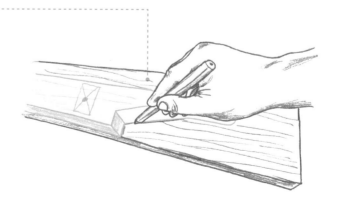

8

Mark out the incremental measurements indicated in the plan on both side rails. For ours, each step is $9\frac{1}{8}$in (23.2cm) from the next, measured along the side rail (because we divided the height of our platform into 12 even steps), so the incremental distance is $9\frac{1}{8} + 9\frac{1}{8} + 9\frac{1}{8} + ...$ (23.2 + 23.2 + 23.2 + ...). This will vary according to the height of your platform.

9

Working from the lower end of the side rail, set an angle of 72.4 degrees in the sliding bevel and draw a line at this angle at every one of the points you have just marked. Take one of the steps and offer it up beneath the line, with the top face level with the line. Draw around the step with a pencil and repeat this procedure for each line.

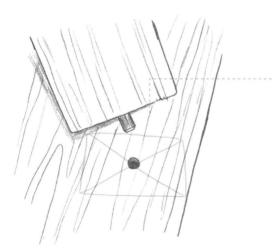

10

Pencil in the diagonals from corner to corner, creating a cross in the rectangles you have just drawn, to find the center of each. Now use a $\frac{1}{2}$in (12mm) drill bit to drill a vertical hole at each of these marked midpoints, making each hole at least as deep as half the length of the dowels.

11

Mark up the diagonals in exactly the same way at both ends of all the steps, as you did for the side rails in step 10.

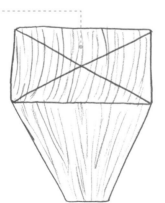

12

Round off the edges of the steps with the router. Don't do this in advance or the midpoints will be more difficult to mark out.

Check to see if all the steps fit and the holes are drilled deep enough.

13

Smear a little glue around all the dowel holes and insert the dowels into both sides of the steps. Insert these into the holes in one of the side rails until each one is seated.

14

Lay the second side rail on top and insert each dowel in turn into the holes until the side rail lies flush with all the steps. This is a job for two people, ideally. Check that all the steps are still at the right angle before clamping the side rails together with several screw clamps.

Take the ½in (12mm) drill bit and make a hole ¾in (2cm) beneath the third and the ninth steps from the bottom, going through both side rails. Thread a 21¼in (54cm) length of threaded rod through these holes, and add a washer and nut at each end.

Screw each step to the side rails with an additional screw (for safety), tighten everything up and you are done! Let the glue dry overnight, and only then remove the clamps.

What to do on site

15

At the far end of the platform there will be an obvious gap in the handrail, where the ladder should go. Lean the ladder up against this gap until the right-angled rebates at the top butt up against the underside of the platform. Once the ladder is seated against the platform, mark the points on the ground where the ladder is standing. Trim off the bottom of the ladder, leaving it "hovering" about 2–4in (5–10cm) above the ground. It will eventually stand on small feet, and this clearance from the ground will also protect it from damp. Dig some small footings about 8in (20cm) in diameter and 16in (40cm) deep at the points marked on the ground.

16

Screw L-shaped post anchors to the inner sides of the side rails. The screws of choice here are #12×2in (6×50mm) waferhead screws (or the thickest screws you can find). If the post anchors are too big, angle grind them back as required, sealing the cut edges with zinc galvanizing spray to prevent rust in the future.

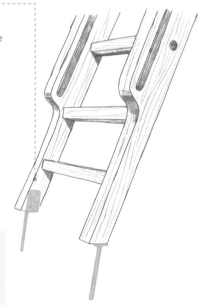

☞ When clamping your newly glued ladder, place bits of scrap wood over the jaws of the clamps so they don't mark the side rails.

17

Mix the concrete in the usual way and pour it into the holes up to the brim. After you've smeared the rebates with glue, insert the post anchors into the concrete so that the ladder rebates are once more properly seated against the platform. Screw the rebates to the platform (#12×4¾in/6×120mm screws should do the trick). Rest the bottom of the ladder on battens, boards, or wooden blocks laid across the footings so that it is held securely in place until the foundations have set.

You will now have as long as the setting time to inspect the treehouse from below. Nobody should be allowed up or there is a risk that the post anchors will work themselves loose in the wet concrete.

It's not absolutely essential to concrete in the ladder and attach it with screws, but this way it will be much more robust and more protected against ground moisture. Alternatively, you can just lean it against the treehouse when you need to use it and take it away when you are out and about, thereby protecting the treehouse from unwelcome guests.

Now that the outer shell is in place, let's turn to the inside. What would a treetop nest be without a beautiful floor, insulation for spontaneous pajama parties, or cozy furniture? If your custom-made treehouse does not fit mass-produced goods from a certain Scandinavian furniture store, and that collector's item from the flea market looks strangely out of place up in the treetops, don't despair. Here we offer ideas for creating custom-made furniture that fits organically into its surroundings and will add both charm and comfort to your new treehouse.

5

Building
the Interior

5.1
Floorboards

The upper story is still in need of a floor. There's really not much else to say on the matter, so let's get on with it!

MATERIALS

- Interlocking (tongue-and-groove) floorboards
- #5×2in (3.2×50mm) countersunk stainless-steel screws
- Floor trim, 1¼in (3cm) thick and 1⅜in (3.5cm) high

What to do in the workshop

1

Cut the floorboards to the requisite length; in our case, it was 126cm (49½in). Subtract about an inch (a couple of centimeters) from the width of the room all around to give a little leeway and you won't have to force the boards in.

What to do on site

2

Start by laying the first board at the front by the window: this will be a straight starting point.

 Kids who can use a cordless drill correctly can help you fit the floorboards and then the trim. They can also start thinking about the interior decor for the upper floor and begin to gather fixtures and fittings, such as pillows (cushions), books, and pictures.

3

Lay the board with the groove flush to the wall, leaving ⅜in (1cm) of clearance to the walls on both the right and left sides. Sink a flooring screw as close to the wall as possible into each joist underneath the board. Sink a flooring screw into the groove above every joist, driving the screw away from you into the board at an angle of about 45 degrees. The screw must ultimately be fully seated in the board for you to fit the next one flush. Be careful during this step that the groove doesn't snap off. Practice beforehand on a piece of scrap board.

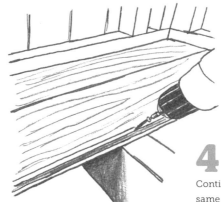

4

Continue with each board in the same way, using a hammer and a bit of scrap wood to knock each board flush with the previous one before screwing it into place. When you reach the opening in the floor for the ladder, cut the boards to the appropriate length.

5

To finish off, fit floor trim around the edges. Rip some trim to size and cut miters at each end for a perfect fit. Fix it with countersunk screws to the wall beams behind. If your floorboards are 1in (2.5cm) thick, the top edge of the floor trim should now be the same height as the wall beams behind it.

Here's how the whole thing will look once it's finished. Install a mattress, add a few throw pillows (cushions), and relax!

5.2
Fixtures and fittings

Your treehouse is up, nosy squirrels have tested it out by leaping around on it, and the first birds are applying to be tenants.

The interior furnishings and fittings that will make it a cozy nest are yet to come, however, giving you free rein and endless creative choices.

These will depend on the intended purposes of the treehouse: different furniture is of course required for a play house than for a study or guest bedroom. There is limited space in a treehouse, so multipurpose furniture is a good option. We recommend some books on woodworking in the Sources section (page 169), and easy-to-follow tutorials for furniture are available online.

Here we describe the basics: a table and bench you can build yourself. Allow a whole day to complete these; you won't require a second pair of hands, but for the sake of safety, please work with another person.

Two simple options for homemade furniture

Your treehouse has an entirely wooden frame and no inner cladding, leaving you plenty of places where you can screw things to the walls. If you want a built-in seat or bed, you already have some of the feet you will need; screw the furniture to the wall and you will only have to build supports at the front.

Furniture such as that shown opposite is very easy to make. Since you've just built an entire treehouse, you should be able to source all the required materials (except for the tabletop) from offcuts.

The principle for the two pieces shown here is about the same: a mitered frame supporting a single piece of ply (for the tabletop) or planed boards (for the seat and backrest of the bench). The legs and supporting framework of both are constructed from offcuts of 2×4in (6×6cm) spruce battens.

  As in previous sections, kids can help with measuring and marking. Their creativity will also be needed, of course, to make sure the treehouse remains their favourite hideaway for years to come. Simple furniture and other items are generally small-scale projects that can often be done with hand tools.

Bench

There's just room to fit a bench against the wall between the door and the window seat. We installed ours level with the wall joist in the oriel window, i.e. 14¼in (36cm) high, measured from the floor to the top edge of the 2×2in (6×6cm) batten. Then, when the bench frame is boarded out (as with the window seat on page 117), the seats are level. Screw the boards in place.

To fix the backrest to the wall, you will need a batten at the right height. Cut two 2×2in (6×6cm) battens to size and cut a miter of 27.4 degrees at one end of both. Install them at a height of 32½in (82.5cm), measuring from the floor to their top edges, and board out as with the seat.

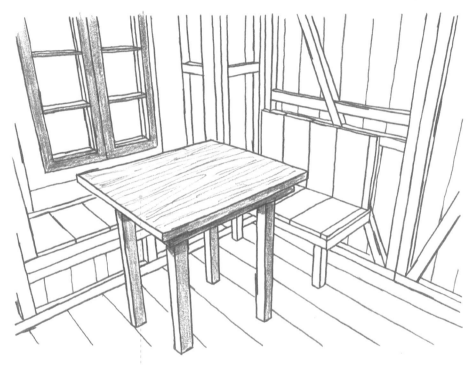

Table

Cut the plywood panel to size, or have it cut at the hardware store. To neaten the edges, glue narrow (¼x1¼in/6×30mm) strips of wood all around; rip them from larch boards and cut a 45-degree miter at each end to bring them down to size. Glue them to the edges of the panel, leaving the strips overlapping by ¼in (5mm) at the top, then clamp and leave to set overnight.

Make the supporting frame from four 2×2in (6×6cm) battens, then glue it to the underside of the tabletop, about 1½in (4cm) in from the edges. (It's fine to sink screws through from the top of the panel; later you can fill the holes with wood filler and sand it flat.) Cut four legs to a length of 30in (76cm) and screw them into the corners of the frame.

5.3
Insulation

Your treehouse might be finished, but you certainly aren't! You want to keep on building, using the experience you've gained to make this attractive place (created with your own bare hands) even more beautiful.

As a first step, insulation allows you to use the treehouse comfortably year round. There are many different types, but in our opinion, the only options for serious consideration involve products made from natural materials. Among the most reliable are fiber insulation boards, which can be made from wood, reeds, flax, and hemp, among other materials. These are available in various qualities, but make sure they are compostable; you can then be sure that they contain no harmful substances. Consult the manufacturer's instructions for detailed guidance on how to use them.

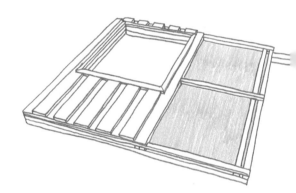

Roof

You should ideally insulate the roof before finishing the treehouse, to avoid having to work overhead. The best approach is to insulate from outside, applying the insulation on top of the roof boards. Double up the rafters on the roof boards and screw these to the rafters running beneath them, fitting the fiber insulation boards in the gaps between. Fit another layer of boards on top, lay a waterproof membrane over them, staple it in place, and continue as described in section 4.10.

Floor

The principle of insulating the floor is the same as for the walls and roof, but without battens. Lay a waterproof membrane on the baseboards, leaving a few inches/centimeters of overlap up the walls all the way around. Glue the seams, then lay floor battens, leaving just enough clearance for a fiber insulation board after each one. Screw the battens to the platform joists beneath where possible. Now lay the floor as described in section 5.1.

Walls

Wood-fiber insulation boards 2in (6cm) thick are ideally suited to fit between the 2×2in (6×6cm) spruce joists we used for our wall framing. Fit the insulation, cover with your choice of cladding (see 4.5), and you are done!

The wall structure for insulated walls looks a little different from that of our treehouse. In such cases, we recommend fixing the interior cladding to battens to ensure good ventilation behind it. To achieve this, cover the insulated wall frame with a membrane (ideally a breathable one), then fit the battens, followed by cladding on top (see illustration above).

5.4
Interior cladding

If you insulate the walls of your treehouse, you must also clad them inside.

The best option here is interlocking (tongue-and-groove) boards, which are made from a variety of woods and available in different thicknesses. Make sure at the planning stage of your own treehouse that the wall framing has enough points at which you can fit the interior cladding; ideally, you should be able to attach it at intervals of no more than 28in (70cm). Profiled boards made from spruce, pine, Douglas fir, arolla pine, and Scotch (Scots) pine, among others, are suitable for use as interior cladding.

Floor

Floorboards are also available as easily laid interlocking (tongue-and-groove) boards. These are usually a little thicker than the interior cladding boards, and spruce, pine, oak, ash, maple, and beech, among others, are all suitable for flooring.

No self-respecting treehouse
should be without an escape route,
such as a secret hatch in the floor
leading to a climbing net, for example,
or a firefighter's pole. We have put
together a selection of the most
popular special features. Even if
your project is not destined to be
a play house, you are bound to find
some gems that will make your
treehouse even more of a treasure.

6

Special Features

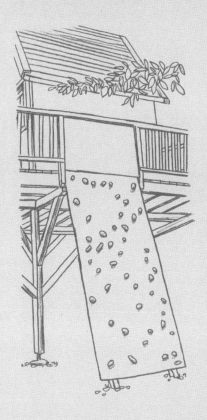

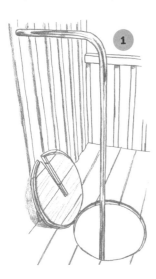

Bike elevator

An even more demanding project: a bike-operated treehouse lift, designed by Ethan Schlussler in the United States. See his YouTube video explaining how it works. It's really cool!

Bucket lift

Can be used to haul up supplies, books, and occasionally even homework. A home-concocted ropeway using old bicycle parts is a particular challenge.

Climbing net

A climbing net is an ideal way to get aboard a treehouse; they are available in a wide range of colors and sizes, and should be secured with screws at the top and concreted into place at the bottom.

Climbing wall 3

The holds are available from sports retailers and/or climbing stores. Screw them to a large larch panel and you have a climbing wall. Design any kind of route, from My First Climbing Wall to death-defying overhangs.

Firefighter's pole 1

Popular with children of all ages, particularly when combined with a hatch in the floor. Poles are available in various lengths, ready for screwing in place at the top and concreting in at the bottom. You can also build one yourself out of stainless-steel piping, but make sure to fix it securely in place.

Zip line/flying fox

The quickest and most enjoyable way of getting from A to B in your own backyard, ideally zooming from the platform to a distant tree. If yours happens to go over a lake, let go halfway and fall in.

Hatch

A hatch or trapdoor that lifts up and down offers privacy. If it's also lockable, it provides protection against uninvited guests.

Individual mechanisms and gadgets

Be creative and let the ideas flow. Every detail that isn't part of the plan will make your treehouse unique.

Knotted climbing rope 2

All you need here is a rope and a screw hook: simple and effective.

Nest swing

These are available in open and closed versions, the latter being almost a little treehouse in itself. Hang it underneath the platform or from a neighboring tree.

Secret compartment

No illustration or it wouldn't be secret! A discreet little door, somewhere in the wall. Or behind it.

 Inspect the treehouse with your children, figure out what it is missing, and find a good place for a secret hiding place or a nest swing.

Rope bridge

The perfect way to connect two platforms of the same height. Chains or steel cables are good options for secure installation and are ideal if you want to fit boards on top. Simpler rope bridges are less complicated to install and not as comfortable to walk across, but they offer more of an adventure.

Slide

Yet another classic, and a very popular escape route when parents suddenly show up—especially in its most elaborate incarnation, the tunnel slide.

Swing

A classic, and particularly enjoyable if positioned with a good view of the treehouse: in a neighboring tree, for example. One board, two ropes, job done.

Hammock

This is another classic, and a good way to use the protected space underneath the treehouse.

Sources

Has your thirst for knowledge about treehouses been awakened? Would you like to know more about trees, build your own treetop bed, or playfully prepare your child(ren) for the project? Our list of suggested reading features a wide variety of useful literature on trees, wood, and treehouses, from tree identification manuals to illustrated guides and children's books.

Please support your local bookstore and ask them to order the book(s) of your choice. In many cases, your order will be ready the next day and you can start reading right away. Bookstore staff will often also have good tips for other books that will help with your new thirst for tree knowledge!

We have compiled this list as best we can, but it makes no claim to completeness. Happy exploring!

Tree identification

Tony Russell, Catherine Cutler, and Martin Walters, *The World Encyclopedia of Trees: A Reference and Identification Guide to 1,300 of the World's Most Significant Trees*, Lorenz Books, 2020
> A beautifully illustrated and uniquely comprehensive standard reference work on hundreds of tree species from all over the world.

Margot Spohn and Dr Roland Spohn, *Trees of Britain and Europe* (Black's Nature Guide), A. & C. Black, 2008
> Clearly laid-out tree identification book featuring more than 350 trees and shrubs from all over Europe.

Interesting facts about trees

Dr Qing Li, *Shinrin-Yoku, the Art and Science of Forest Bathing: How Trees Can Help You Find Health and Happiness*, Penguin Life, 2018
> This is the place to look up how nature therapy is practiced, how you can bring the healing scents of the forest into your home, and which houseplants are particularly good for your health.

Claus Mattheck, *Stupsi Explains the Tree: A Hedgehog Teaches the Body Language of Trees*, Karlsruhe Institute of Technology, 1999
> A book about tree health recommended by treehouse-builders and arborists (tree surgeons) alike. It might seem like a children's book, but it is a comprehensible work with simple explanations addressing complex topics—suitable for young and old!

Claus Mattheck, *Updated Field Guide for Visual Tree Assessment*, Karlsruhe Institute of Technology, 2007
> A soundly researched and easy-to-read guide to tree health. Learn the body language of trees and fungi, and understand their warning signals.

Nalini Nadkarni, *Between Earth and Sky: Our Intimate Connections to Trees*, University of California Press, 2009
> This book, by a world-famous tree expert, explains unexpected links between trees from all over the world.

David Suzuki, Wayne Grady, and Robert Bateman, *Tree: A Life Story*, Greystone Books, 2004
> Seven centuries in the life of a Douglas fir condensed into one book, affording an understanding of how everything in nature is connected, and how essential trees are for humankind and the natural world. After reading this, you will bow before every tree.

Peter Wohlleben, *The Hidden Life of Trees: What They Feel, How They Communicate: Discoveries from a Secret World*, Penguin Allen Lane, 2016
> That trees exchange messages, feel pain, and have memory are just some of the secrets revealed in this book by the renowned forester Peter Wohlleben.

Beautiful and informative books about trees

Jennifer Davis, *100 Things to Do in a Forest*, Laurence King, 2020
   So I have a treehouse now—but what do I do in a forest? Build a bivouac, start a forest diary, or do some nature therapy—this magical illustrated book has countless suggested answers to this question. Also of interest to kids.

Jonathan Drori and Lucille Clerc, *Around the World in 80 Trees*, Laurence King, 2018
   Alongside exceptionally beautiful illustrations, this book presents fascinating and informative facts about the world's great trees.

Jen Green, *The Magic and Mystery of Trees*, Dorling Kindersley Kids/ Royal Horticultural Society, 2019
   The miracle of trees with all their many facets, from roots to treetop, with informative, concise, and amusing illustrations.

Kevin Hobbs and David West, *The Story of Trees and How They Changed the Way We Live*, Laurence King, 2020
   A beautifully visualized and informative cultural history of trees.

Cesare Leonardi and Franca Stagi, *The Architecture of Trees*, Abrams & Chronicle Books, 2019
   One for tree-lovers: large-format, hand-drawn black-and-white illustrations of 212 trees over the course of the four seasons.

John Lewis-Stempel, *The Wood: The Life and Times of Cockshutt Wood*, Doubleday, 2018
   Live in a forest from spring to winter with one of England's best nature writers, who crafts pictures with an informative yet deeply poetic sensibility.

Steve Marsh, *The Tree: The Book that Transforms into a Work of Art*, Welbeck Publishing, 2018
   A visually entrancing journey through the world's most majestic trees; chock-full of informative stories and accompanied by beautiful press-out illustrations.

Fiona Stafford, *The Long, Long Life of Trees*, Yale University Press, 2017
   How have trees been represented in art, history, commerce, and folklore over time? Tree-lover Fiona Stafford offers a personal commentary as she takes you on an exciting excursion into the long life of trees.

Treehouses

Paula Henderson and Adam Mornement, *Treehouses*, Frances Lincoln, 2005
   As well as finding out about historic, planned, public, and private treehouses, along with a wealth of tips about treehouse-building, you will learn all about the history of treehouses from this book.

Philip Jodidio, *Tree Houses: Fairy-tale Castles in the Air*, Taschen, 2020
   This large-format volume brings together 50 extraordinary treehouses from every continent.

Sybille Kramer, *Green, Hidden and Above: The Most Exceptional Treehouses*, Braun Publishing, 2015
   From an adventure treehouse for children to hideaways in the heart of nature to a treehouse hotel, this illustrated volume presents a collection of exciting treehouses to inspire your own project.

Alain Laurens, Daniel Dufour, Ghislain André, and La Cabane Perchée, *Dream Treehouses: Extraordinary Designs from Concept to Completion*, Abrams, 2016
   La Cabane Perchée presents 40 of its most beautiful and habitable nests in treetops all over Europe and the United States.

Pete Nelson, *Treehouses of the World*, Abrams 2004, and *New Treehouses of the World*, Abrams, 2009
   International tours of new treehouses in many different cultures and settings.

Pete Nelson, *Be in a Treehouse: Design, Construction, Inspiration*, Abrams, 2014
   In addition to discovering the world's most original treehouses, here you will find out how a treehouse is created, from initial idea to final floorboard.

Woodworking

Paul Forrester, *The Woodworker's Technique Bible: The Essential Illustrated Reference*, Search Press, 2021
   A step-by-step practical guide, from advice on buying the right resources and tools to basic woodworking techniques and ideas for projects.

Phillip Gardener and Andy Standing, *Practical Weekend Projects for Woodworkers: 35 Projects to Make for Every Room of Your Home*, IMM Lifestyle, 2018
   An ideal resource for any treehouse-builder, full of practical ideas for things to do with offcuts, whether for a toolbox, a folding stool, or a weathercock.

Christopher Stuart, *DIY Furniture: A Step-by-step Guide*, Laurence King 2011, and *DIY Furniture 2: A Step-by-step Guide*, Laurence King, 2014
   Amazing ideas for simple ways to make domestic items using materials available from any hardware store.

Woodwork: The Complete Step-by-step Manual: Tools, Techniques, Woods, Projects, Dorling Kindersley, 2020
   This comprehensive workbook features 28 different projects (including furniture) for all levels of ability, with more than 2,800 illustrations and extensive explanations of tools.

Technical reference

Black & Decker, *The Complete Guide to Wiring*, 8th ed., Cool Springs Press, 2022

A comprehensive and up-to-date guide from this most iconic of tool brands, complete with 2021–24 electrical codes. Specific to the United States, but with plenty of information that is invaluable elsewhere.

Chris Kitcher, *Wiring and Lighting*, 2nd ed., Crowood Press, 2020

A comprehensive guide to home wiring, with reference to UK regulations.

www.diydoctor.org.uk

Advice on all aspects of home construction projects, including a full section on electrical work, and useful guidance on what is and isn't suitable for the home electrician to carry out. UK-focused.

Other recommended reading

Vicky Allan and Anna Deacon, *For the Love of Trees*, Black & White Publishing, 2020

A beautifully photographed book telling the stories of people who love trees, why trees are important to them, and why trees matter to all humans.

Italo Calvino, *The Baron in the Trees*, Harvest, 1959

The classic treehouse book. One day the 12-year-old Baron withdraws from his family and decides that, henceforth, he will live in the trees.

Artur Cisar-Erlach, *The Flavor of Wood: In Search of the Wild Taste of Trees from Smoke and Sap to Root and Bark*, Abrams, 2019

The author, a woodland ecologist and food expert, conjures up a forest on your tongue and takes you on a journey of culinary discovery all around the world.

Sally Coulthard, *Biophilia: You + Nature + Home: A Handbook for Bringing the Natural World into Your Life*, Kyle Books, 2020

Bring the interior decoration of your treehouse a little closer to nature and boost your well-being as you do so. A beautifully produced book with inspiring contents.

Lars Mytting, *Norwegian Wood: Chopping, Stacking and Drying Wood the Scandinavian Way*, MacLehose Press, 2015

A much-recommended, amusing, and easy-to-read volume with new background knowledge on the subject of firewood. Impossible to put down until you've finished it.

Children's books
2–4 YEARS AND OLDER

Christian Broutin, *My First Discoveries: Trees*, Moonlight, 2010

A great starting point for young botanists.

Tracy Cottingham, *Lift and Look: Trees*, Bloomsbury Activity Books, 2021

A lift-the-flap book to introduce little ones to trees, from the Royal Botanic Gardens, Kew, London.

Emily Haworth-Booth, *The Last Tree*, Pavilion Children's, 2020

An important parable from an award-winning author, illustrator, and climate activist.

Minna Lacey and Bao Luu, *Look Inside the Woods*, Usborne, 2021

A lift-the-flap book for young nature lovers to discover hidden animals and fun facts.

Neal Layton, *The Tree: An Environmental Fable*, Walker Books, 2017

What happens when people decide to cut down a tree and use it to build a house? A simple picture book with a strong message about the way wildlife and humans can coexist.

Britta Teckentrup, *Tree: A Peek-through Picture Book*, Doubleday Books for Young Readers, 2016

A delightful pop-up book for the youngest "readers," introducing them to the animals that live in and around trees.

4-6 YEARS AND OLDER

Sue Fliess and Miki Sakamoto, *Let's Build*, Two Lions, 2014
> A parent and child build together, from making plans to visiting a hardware store and enjoying the finished creation. Perfect for anyone planning to build with their children.

Gail Gibbons, *Tell Me, Tree: All About Trees for Kids*, Little, Brown, 2002
> A delightful oversized book explaining and celebrating all parts of the tree and offering ideas for crafty projects, such as pressing leaves and making bark rubbings.

Carter Higgins and Emily Hughes, *Everything You Need for a Treehouse*, Chronicle Books, 2018
> A magical illustrated children's book written in rhyme about building fantastic treehouses; particularly powerful inspiration for encouraging ideas.

Lars Klinting, *Harvey the Carpenter*, Kingfisher Books, 2005
> The workshop is in such chaos that Harvey the beaver decides to build himself a toolbox. An educational story with charming pictures, detailed descriptions, and building instructions.

René Mettler, *Woods and Forests*, Moonlight Publishing, 2013
> A beautifully illustrated book about the importance of trees and forests—and the plants, insects, and animals that inhabit them.

Gerda Muller, *A Year Around the Great Oak*, Floris Books, 2019
> A beautifully illustrated new printing of the first edition of this title, from 1991. Expert knowledge woven into an entrancing story about a 300-year-old oak, its denizens, and the surrounding natural world.

Piotr Socha and Wojciech Grajkowski, *The Book of Trees*, Thames & Hudson, 2018
> This large picture book includes the gamut of tree species and deals with everything from prehistoric trees to the use of trees as instruments, plus stories of tree monsters. Best for age 5 and older, but even at the age of 2, our son loved the illustrations.

6-8 YEARS AND OLDER

Shira Boss and Jamey Christoph, *Up in the Leaves: The True Story of the Central Park Treehouses*, Sterling Publishing, 2018
> The story of the boy who built secret treehouses in Central Park, New York.

Kirsteen Robson, Sam Smith, and Stephanie Fizer Coleman, *Trees to Spot* (Usborne Minis), Usborne, 2019
> Pop this little book in your pocket and identify every species! As children discover and identify each one, they can record it in the identification table with a sticker.

Doug Stowe, *The Guide to Woodworking with Kids: Craft Projects to Develop the Lifelong Skills of Young Makers*, Blue Hills Press, 2020
> A primer of basic carpentry skills through easy-to-make projects—and just as helpful for parents, guardians, and teachers hoping to give children a solid grounding in woodwork.

Naomi Walmsley and Dan Westall, *Forest School Adventure: Outdoor Skills and Play for Children*, GMC, 2018
> Let your child(ren) create leaf prints for treehouse pillows (cushions), and tree spirits or bird feeders from forest materials, while you work away on the roof truss and keep an envious eye on them. This book contains a wealth of exciting suggestions for forest activities.

Peter Wohlleben, *Can You Hear the Trees Talking?: Discovering the Hidden Life of the Forest*, Greystone Kids, 2020
> A refreshing read, answering the most unusual, funniest, and most entertaining questions about trees and their inhabitants.

8-10 YEARS AND OLDER

Nicola Davies and Lorna Scobie, *The Wonder of Trees*, Hodder Children's Books, 2019
> Colorful, lavish, and highly informative. A large-format book of hidden forest treasures that is an engaging read to boot.

Gina Ingoglia, *The Tree Book for Kids and their Grown-ups*, Brooklyn Botanic Garden, 2013
> The answers to all sorts of tree-related questions, featuring 33 of the trees that grow in North America. For readers of all ages.

Hubert Reeves, Nelly Boutinot, and Daniel Casanave, *Hubert Reeves Explains: Forests*, Europe Comics, 2019
> An entertaining forest comic that also offers valuable expertise. A class listens as the Canadian atomic physicist and astrophysicist Reeves explains our ecosystem, why forests are so important for us, and what we can do to preserve them.

Charlotte Voake, *A Little Guide to Trees*, Eden Children's Books, 2009
> A tree identification book brimming with lovingly designed illustrations that will playfully inspire you to look at trees more closely.

Websites

www.asca-consultants.org
Tree-focused advice and resources from the American Society of Consulting Arborists.

www.baumbaron.de
Our most beautiful projects are available as inspiration for your treehouse on our treehouse workshop website, with texts written by Miriam. German and English.

www.treehouseblog.com
Our blog contains lots of articles about treehouses, along with FAQs on treehouse-building. You are welcome to ask us questions relating to your project or send us photos of your finished treehouse to consider for publication on the blog. We are also delighted to receive book tips or other recommendations.

www.thetreehouse.shop
Helpful tips for treehouse-building and suppliers of the tree attachment bolts we used. German and English.

www.nelsontreehouse.com
Let the projects completed by the treehouse pioneer Pete Nelson and his team lend you wings.

www.treehouses.com
The treehouse pioneer Michael Garnier welcomes you to the Out 'n' About Treehouse Resort in Oregon. The annual Worldwide Treehouse Conference is held here, with treehouse-builders and fans from all over the world meeting to swap notes. The site also has construction plans that you can download.

www.trees.org.uk
Are you not quite sure your tree is entirely healthy? Here you'll find a comprehensive directory of tree surgeons all over the UK, as well as help and advice.

Suppliers

If possible, cultivate a personal contact in your chosen supplier or store so that you can ask questions and find out where the materials come from. There is no substitute for good advice tailored to your needs.

www.activegarden.co.uk
Sells play components, such as swings, basketball nets, rope ladders, and even a flagpole. For creative additions to your treehouse!

store.beinatree.com
Pete Nelson's online store, for everything from high-quality TABs and climbing kits to tree-branded baseball caps.

www.cacoonworld.com
Manufacturers of cozy nest swings/hanging tents—an improvement for any tree, even without a treehouse.

www.classichandtools.com
A small, independent supplier of hand tools, based in Suffolk, UK.

www.diy.com
The website of B&Q, one of the UK's most popular home-improvement and tool stores. Stocks the major brands of tools and equipment, including Makita, DeWalt, and Bosch, as well as lumber (timber).

www.flints.co.uk
A British theatrical supplier, but well worth a visit for its range of rigging fixtures, ladders, safety equipment, electrical supplies, and more.

www.freeworker.de/en
You will find everything your treehouse-building heart could desire in this store, including climbing gear and pulley blocks with brakes. There is also a large selection of reference works on trees and tree care.

www.holzschindeln.de/en/home
Wooden shingles of varying qualities, and tips on how to fit them.

www.homebase.co.uk
A popular, mainstream DIY and tool store in the UK selling all the major brands and offering wood as well.

www.lowes.com
One of the largest home-improvement retailers in the world, with an extensive building supplies section.

www.onlineplaygrounds.co.uk
Swings, slides, rope slides, firefighter's poles, and plenty more.

www.rockler.com
A giant US store with a large selection of top-quality professional tools; also offers practical advice.

safetynet365.com
Climbing nets and protective netting made to size.

www.travisperkins.co.uk
A one-stop UK store for the serious woodworker, with tools, lumber (timber), fixings, flooring, and sheet materials.

www.thetreehouse.shop
Here you can order all the hardware we used, such as the GTS Allstar tree attachment bolt.

www.treehousesupplies.com
For treehouse-specific hardware, including TABs.

www.treetopbuilders.net
This specialist US treehouse-building firm also offers professional-grade parts and materials for the home builder.

www.woodcraft.com
One of the USA's oldest and largest suppliers of woodworking tools.

Index

Acknowledgments

We would like to thank from the bottom of our hearts all those who gave us their support as we built the treehouse and wrote this book—first and foremost our moms and dads, who always encouraged us to do what we really wanted to. Johannes Schelle, because working with you at Baumbaron is the greatest thing you can do for money. Rainer Rohm, Tim Gemsjäger, Vitus Wahlländer, Paula Töpper, Josef Hitsch, Sebastian Hage, and Felix Herzberg, because we make such an amazing team. Extra thanks to Vitus for further refinement of the tree attachment bolt. Gabriel Faber for your enthusiastic support, Casey Clapp for the guide to tree health, and the Davidoff family and their daughter Leni for the opportunity to build on their beautiful land, and for their support during the treehouse build. Many thanks indeed to Jo Lightfoot, Zara Larcombe, John Parton, Andrew Roff, Rosanna Fairhead, Alex Coco, and everyone else involved at Laurence King Publishing for giving us the opportunity to share our knowledge with others and to make the world a better place with lots of treehouses. We would like to thank David Sparshott for the beautiful illustrations in this book, which have made the procedures a lot easier to understand.

In addition, Christopher sends deeply felt gratitude all the way to America, to Pete Nelson, for everything you have shown him. Also to Judy, Emily, Charlie and Henry Nelson, Bubba and Anna Smith, Daryl McDonald and Nicola Temple, Rusty, Jake Jacob and Lela Hilton, Ian Weedman, Sarah Jay Knauss, Seanix Junker, Kai and Jenny Nybro, Ben Smith, Michael Garnier, and Scott Baker, for the unforgettable times and all the future memories. Last, but not least, Miriam would like to sincerely thank Jürgen Nerger for having opened the door to writing for her.

Laurence King Publishing is grateful to Dan Jackson, Pete Nelson, and Richard Thorne for their contribution to the making of this book.

About the authors

CHRISTOPHER RICHTER has been building treehouses professionally since 2003, and since 2010 with Johannes Schelle at the firm Baumbaron, based in Tegernsee, Germany. He has built more than 100 treehouses as a designer and planner at Baumbaron, and the company has completed more than 200 projects overall. Christopher learned his trade with Pete Nelson in the United States, and they have shared a deep friendship since his first visit in 2003.

MIRIAM RÜGGEBERG is a freelance editor and blogger who has been sharing her fascination for treehouses in her *Treehouseblog* since 2014. She has been spreading the treehouse gospel across the internet with well-researched contributions on all aspects of the subject, to the delight of an ever-expanding treehouse community. Other writings of hers about treehouses have been published on the Baumbaron website, in books, and in (online) magazines.

www.baumbaron.de
www.treehouseblog.com

PETE NELSON Pete fell in love with treehouses as a child, and has since created hundreds of treehouses around the world with his design and build firm, Nelson Treehouse and Supply. He has published several books on the art and science of treehouse-building, and has shared many of his builds with global audiences as the star of the hit Animal Planet television series *Treehouse Masters*.

www.nelsontreehouse.com

Download the construction plan for our treehouse here.

2: Above
On a wooded site, make your visitors work hard by building the entrance separately on a nearby tree. A spiral staircase and rope bridge increase the challenge.

1: Previous page
What could be better to encourage exploration than a rope bridge?

3: Opposite
Leni's completed treehouse—a source of enjoyment and great pride for years to come.

4: Above

This narrow treehouse is fitted into a small gap between trees on this wooded hillside. The steeply pitched roof and dark-stained walls give it a Scandinavian vibe.

5: Opposite

A gable end with inset window allows extra light into this shaded treehouse.

**6, 7: Previous pages
and opposite, top**
The occupants of this magnificent
treehouse are spoilt for choice
when it comes to entering and
leaving their woodland domain.

8: Opposite, bottom
A zip line offers the ultimate
in sharp exits.

9: Above
The safely netted walls of this
rope bridge still allow a sense of
adventure to prevail.

10: Opposite

A simple trapdoor is an easy way to reach an upper story. Add a removable ladder and you can be choosy about the company you keep in your treehouse.

11: Above

A cover with a slot cut through allows the firefighter's pole to be made safe when necessary.

12: Overleaf

A timber-clad interior needs very little furnishing to make it feel cozy and homey.

13: Above
Creating a reading nook will make
sure you get hours of enjoyment
from your treehouse.

14: Opposite
What bliss to wake up in
a room like this, to the sound
of birds singing.

15: Overleaf
One of the more unusual
treehouse features—but what
a talking point! This bicycle-
powered elevator was designed
and built by Ethan Schlussler for
his treehouse in Idaho.